Endorsements

From His Holiness, the XIVth Dalai Lama
"This book by Professor Michael Kuhar focuses on many important ideas. He describes how a broader awareness of human nature, derived from scientific enquiry, combined with the practice of fairness and compassion leads to friendlier relations with others. He also point out that for ethics to be effective they have to involve not only thinking, but action too. If we act on our sense of compassion, it not only benefits others, but us as well. There is a great deal in this book to think about and to put into effect. If we can do that we will succeed in making a more peaceful, more compassionate society."

From Paul Root Wolpe, Ph.D., Director, Center for Ethics, Emory University
"Drawing from psychological, educational, and other professional literature, Michael Kuhar reminds us how much of our lives are spent around colleagues, and how compelling is the benefit and the obligation to learn how to treat them fairly and with intention. Suggesting strategies for handling situations many of us confront every day, Kuhar provides a guide that can make our professional lives easier and more fulfilling, and just might spill over into our relationships with our family and friends as well. I hope that the idea of "collegial Ethics" becomes a regular part of the conversation in institutions of higher education, corporations, and other organizations where people work together towards a common goal."

From Ted Ayllon, Ph.D., Behavioral Child-Family Therapist, and author of *Head Strong: A Parenting Survival Kit for Reducing Tension and Building Self-Esteem*

"One of the issues discussed in Kuhar's book is how we acquire the sensitivity and conduct that we call collegiality. It's about how we make it part of our culture. Cost-benefit (or "What's in it for me?") for the individual is the basic component underlying a culture of collegiality, and this book has a plethora of supporting illustrations and novel cases. Kuhar points to the importance of learning the "rules of engagement", or conduct largely through practice. Whether the reader is in a university setting, in business, or in any sports team, s/he will find this book most valuable in learning how to develop and maintain a sense of collaborative assistance and reciprocal caring that increases success and well being."

From Jill Brody, Documentarian and Photographer

"After reading this book I realized that Michael Kuhar was laying out the problem, not with the idea of solving it in every instance, but with the idea of helping people understand its complexity, and of providing suggestions about finding your way through collegial problems. Like all relationships, the ones at work take work of their own. It's a process of learning how to talk, ask questions, and of course, listen—and a process that if done with sincerity, encourages people to become more empathic. Of course, there are people who already are the very embodiment of care and concern for others. But for the rest of us, it is good to have a book like this to remind us that given good will, and a commitment to participate, most of us can learn to be better colleagues, and by extension, kinder and more gentler people all the way around."

From S.J. Enna, Ph.D. Associate Dean for Research and Graduate Training, and Professor, University of Kansas Medical School. Formerly Executive Vice President and Director of Research and Development, Nova Pharmaceutical Corporation

"Professor Kuhar provides thoughtful insight and guidance on the challenges associated with balancing self-interest with our obligations to others. Written from the perspective of an accomplished academician, the principles espoused apply to any type of collaborative endeavor, from marriage to the work environment. The clear explanation of how aspects of human nature suppress altruistic urges and encourage passive or overtly destructive interactions with family, friends and colleagues facilitates the understanding of the recommended corrective measures. While of value to all, this work is recommended for biomedical graduate students, fellows and faculty as part of their training in the responsible conduct of research. As detailed in the text, the awareness and implementation of collegial ethics will improve communication and productivity while fostering personal development and professional success."

From Bebe Forehand, holocaust survivor
«When I was thirteen, my family hid in an attic for more than three years in Antwerp. We were always afraid, and we didn›t have enough to eat. Only as an adult did I fully realize the extent of our deprivation. While we say «Never again.» It could happen again, and it is happening in some ways and places right now. We need to believe in and show our tolerance, compassion and moral courage, and it should start now, in our everyday lives. This book can help us do this.»

From Joanna Fowler, Ph.D. National Medal of Science from President Obama
"This is a gem of a book. Kuhar draws on a keen insight into human nature and how and why we respond to others. He uses real world examples to illustrate how to break out of old molds to establish rewarding interactions with colleagues, friends and with families. This is seriously important. Non-collegial interactions are distracting and disruptive to our families, our workplaces and our government. I found myself thinking about this book a lot and in fact I will be passing my dog-eared copy around."

From Rev. Dr. Edward Frost, Minister
"As a Pastoral Counselor for most of my near-half-century of ministry I have often been sought out by persons whose days were filled with frustration and anxiety out of their experience in the workplace. These problems permeated their lives, often bringing destructive

tension and sometimes tragedy into their relationships. Continuing negative experiences drained pleasure from their work, detracted from their production and quality of contribution and in many cases contributed to the failure of their family and social relations.

So much of this sadness and waste could be avoided or healed by the exercise of collegiality, which Dr. Kuhar astutely defines as *support* and *fairness*. These words are often sprinkled about "how to" books and articles. But, Dr. Kuhar makes an invaluable contribution to the development of healthy and productive collegiality by devoting careful thought to the meaning of these terms—with practical application especially in the often complicated milieu of the workplace.

This is a valuable and highly "usable" book. I strongly recommend it to staff, company leaders—and all of us in relationships we wish to maintain in happiness and deepening value."

From Amy Block Joy, Ph.D., author of *Whistleblower*, and former Director of Food Stamp Nutrition Education Program, California

"I didn't put this book down. Dr Kuhar captures the dilemmas of whistleblowers and the responses of colleagues that make it very difficult. This book points us in the right direction. All of us need the support of our coworkers. This inspiring book also presents a practical framework for creating collegial communities!"

From Dean K. Reger, former HUD official, Washington D.C.

"Professor Kuhar's book, *The Art and Ethics of Being a Good Colleague*, offers not only a useful synopsis of ideas often used in the training of supervisors and managers in the Federal Government, but also numerous insights on human nature in collegial situations. It will be a useful reference and guide for anyone in any work environment. I can think of more than one instance in my experience where having this book as a ready reference may have improved my reaction to a situation. I recommend having a copy of the book close at hand for supervisors and managers in any organization."

From Sandy Roach, CEO of HNR Productions, Inc.

"The topic of Dr. Kuhar's book, *The Art and Ethics of Being a Good Colleague*, is extremely relevant for all of mankind and all human societies. Every organization will benefit from collegial behavior among its members.

Organizations can thrive or perish; even those organizations that are well managed will do better if their members show more than a modicum of respect toward one another. When an organization member (coworker, board member, friend, neighbor, etc.) behaves collegially towards another member they demonstrate their respect for each other.

The ideas put forth in Dr. Kuhar's book offer us tools that will not only help modern organizations but are also essential to the success for our future super-organizations."

The Art and Ethics of Being a Good Colleague

BY MICHAEL J. KUHAR, PhD

Note: The photo of the author on the back cover is modified from Kuhar, M. *The Addicted Brain* FT Press, Upper Saddle River, NJ. 2012.

Copyright © 2013 Michael J. Kuhar Ph.D.
All rights reserved.

ISBN-10: 1479359327
ISBN-13: 9781479359325
Library of Congress Control Number: 2012917781
CreateSpace Independent Publishing Platform,
North Charleston, SC

DEDICATION

This book is dedicated to good colleagues everywhere, and to those whose work helps us understand our human nature and each other.

It is also dedicated to Will and Jake, who will live in the future we give them.

Contents

Introduction   *xiii*

PART I—About Collegiality and Collegial Ethics, and Why Our Very Human Nature Underscores Its Need

Chapter 1. Why Bother With Collegial Ethics?   3
   What Is Collegial Ethics?   3
   A Focus On Collegial Ethics Is Needed   4
   How Does It Work?   5
      Cases: Condolences, Mentoring, and Do No Harm
   Isn't This Just Common Sense?   6
   Collegial Behavior Is Becoming Required   6
   Collegiality Will Improve Our Lives and Institutions   8
   Collegial Ethics Will Counterbalance Accusative Ethics   9
      Case: Erroneous Charge Of Fabricating Data
   We Harvest More When We Tend and Nourish Our Garden   10
   A Nightmare Scenario   10
      Case: Blacklisting
   Do We Have To Give Up Competition?   13
   Successful Precedents   13
   The Bottom Line   14

Chapter 2. Games We Play With Ourselves — 17
    Keep The Peace — 18
        Case: Dating Boyfriend Of Colleague
    What I Do Won't Matter — 19
    Let Them Do It Themselves — 20
    Self-Righteous Judgment — 21
    Excessive Fairness — 22
    Questionable Wisdom — 22
    Giving Disliking Too Much Influence — 23
        Case: Can't Stand A Coworker
    Genuine Paralyzing Fear — 25
    The Bottom Line — 26

Chapter 3. Human Nature, Evolved Instincts and Culture—Can We Change? — 29
    Obedience To authority: The Shocking Work Of Stanley Milgram — 33
    On Emotions and Control — 36
    Are We Truly Rational In Our Responses? — 38
    Moral Reasoning After The Fact — 40
    Attribution Errors — 41
    Say It, Believe It — 42
    The Good Samaritan Experiment: Haste and Failure To Help — 42
        Case: Good Samaritan Study
    Let Somebody Else Do It — 43
        Case: The Genovese Story
    We Are Culturally Diverse — 44
    Bullying: Is It Only For Kids? — 45
        Case: Damage To Others and Restitution
    Can We Change? — 47
    The Bottom Line — 50

Contents   xiii

PART II—Becoming Collegial

Chapter 4. Getting Involved and Being Supportive   59
- Judging The situation   60
- What Will It Cost Me?   62
- How Close Am I To The Situation?   63
- Courage: The Missing Ingredient   64
- Dale Carnegie's Heritage   65
- Tolerance   66
- Institutional Problems   67
- What If *You* Are The One Who Needs Help?   68
- The Bottom Line   68

Chapter 5. Collegial Skills: Language, Guidelines, and Behavior   71
- Practice Being Positive and Uplifting To Others   72
- Develop A Supportive Or Neutral Language   73
  - Case: Cafeteria Talk
- Project A Feeling Of Safety   76
- The Golden Rule   78
- First Do No Harm Or Minimize Harm   79
  - Case: Trophy Hire In Question
- Detraction: The Evil Kind Of Truth   81
- Developing Courage   81
  - Case: To Report Or Not To Report
  - Case: Ugly E-mail
- Giving Credit To Others   86
- Mentoring Others   87
  - Case: Never-On-Time Colleague
  - Case: Making Up Data—Did You Really See It?
  - Case: Is It In My Genes?
- Collegial Ethics and The Boss   91
- The Bottom Line   92

Chapter 6. Collegial Skills: Feelings and Needs   **95**
   Nonviolent Communication (NVC)   95
   Improving Communication   96
      Case: Stealing Ideas
   Responsibility   99
      Case: Kiss Up To The Boss
   Separate What You See from What You Think   100
   Using Empathy   101
   NVC Summary   102
   Conflict Resolution (CR)   102
   Win-Win Strategies   103
   Responses To Conflict   104
   Communicating In CR—Right and Wrong Ways   106
      Case: The Arguing Couple
   Values Differences In CR   110
   CR Summary   110
   Other Approaches   111
   The Bottom Line   111

PART III—Limits, The Future, and Exercises

Chapter 7. Limits Of Collegial Ethics   **117**
   Unwilling and Unworthy Colleagues   117
   Protect Yourself   119
   Not All Colleagues Are Healthy and Able   120
   Collegiality vs. Appropriate Self-Interest   121
      Case: Needy Colleagues At Finals Time
   Are Right and Wrong Always Obvious   123
   Hierarchical Issues   123
      Case: A Boss In A Bind
   Are We Equal Or Not?   125

Secrecy and Lying	126
Access To Training In Collegial Ethics	127
The Bottom Line	127

Chapter 8. Synthesis and Exercises   *129*

List Of Collegial Principles	129
Questions For Discussion	131
Language Styles	132
Listening For Feelings and Needs and Making Requests	133
Win-Win	135
Courage	136
Cases and Questions	137
A Closing Word	147

Supplemental Reading   *151*

Index   *153*

Acknowledgments:

I acknowledge the support and the contributions of several colleagues and friends, including JoAnna Perry who provided edits and obtained permissions, Sandy Roach, Amy Block Joy, Karen Luehrs, Pat Harris, Margita Haberlen, Lloyd Bird, Dorthie Cross, Mary Ann Cree, Ida Cole, and Mary Sherman. I also acknowledge the training in ethics and philosophy given at my college, the University of Scranton, particularly by Thomas M Garrett, and the early focus on tolerance and fairness provided by my father. I am especially indebted to my colleagues at the Center for Ethics of Emory University who made a number of suggestions. They include Paul Root Wolpe, John Banja, Edward Queen II, and Marshall Duke. Support from the Yerkes National Primate Research Center, Emory University, the Georgia Research Alliance, and the National Institutes of Health is also acknowledged.

Introduction

Lift your colleagues up, and they'll lift you up.[1]

❧

Do you want closer relationships with your colleagues but you aren't sure how to achieve that?

Do you know colleagues who could use some help, but you're not sure about getting involved?

Do you say the wrong thing, or don't know what to say?

Are you sometimes unsure about how to be fair?

Do you sometimes feel regretful that you didn't help someone?

Do you sometimes regret not having asked for help?

If you answered yes to any of these questions, this book may help you.

❧

How many of us interact with colleagues (some prefer the word "co-worker") on a daily basis? Certainly almost all of us. Are we comfortable and successful with our colleagues? If not, how do we fix that? Do we have guidelines for collegial interactions that we have thought about?

Responses to these questions will vary because we're all different and in different situations. But there are guidelines that are applicable in a great many settings. This book is about such guidelines and it proposes a philosophy, called Collegial Ethics, [2,3] that will facilitate having rewarding collegial interactions. Although this book obviously focuses on colleagues, it can easily address issues with family and friends as well. Therefore this book can be for everyone. It deals with a seriously important topic that we too often ignore.

Interactions with colleagues are essential, but, amazingly, there is little or no training in what our overall attitudes or interactive techniques should be. Collegial interactions sometimes fail, resulting in a loss of productivity or happiness in the best case, and personal and institutional damage in the worst case. One might say that this training should be included at home and in school in the process of childhood socialization and this may be true. But the world is complex, and this type of early preparation will not be adequate for all situations. Additional material on collegiality is needed; hence this book.

Collegial ethics recommends that you *support and be fair* to your colleagues, not only in the day-to-day humdrum, but also in difficult situations—at least when it is appropriate. Exactly what we mean by support is explained herein. There are certain skills and guidelines that we can learn and practice to help improve collegial relationships and these will be described in the following chapters. For example, a critical skill is developing positive and supportive language. The way we talk to or about another is very powerful, even if we don't realize it. This doesn't mean that you will be constantly "buttering up" your colleagues. It means that you will choose to be positive, fair, and nonjudgmental towards others. Being supportive is not only a means to an end, it is a pleasant way to live. It's a formula for looking at the positive attributes in others and in ourselves instead of looking for the negative. Collegial ethics also means that you will try to accept your colleagues' transgressions with forgiveness and take the time to mentor and help those who need it. Collegial ethics has a strong interest in human nature which underlies how and why we respond to others. Understanding our behavior is part of the foundation of working and interacting with colleagues.

Sometimes we aren't given instructions on how to behave properly in a specific situation, and therefore we don't have the confidence that we are doing it right. We are often told to just "be ourselves" or "just be natural." But what exactly does that mean? What if being natural means that you tell your colleagues or your boss that you can't stand them? "Tell them how you feel about it" is common advice. But we need to be careful when we tell someone how we feel because that could produce a result counter to what we really want. *Feelings* as such are critical among lovers and friends, but they are less critical in the workplace. In the workplace, appropriate behavior that conforms to goals is more important than emotions. Acting appropriately can be a very complex topic, one that can't be easily solved for every situation. Many interpersonal skills, such as being supportive and fair to colleagues, accepting authority, using appropriate assertiveness and conflict resolution, have been developed, and each has its place. A goal of collegial ethics is to prepare us to act appropriately. It is both proactive and reactive. It's not a blueprint for all situations, but it should be very helpful.

Why was this book written? There are several parts to this answer. One is that it is needed, and no more needs to be said about that. A second reason is the interest of the author, which has evolved over many years of learning, experiencing disappointments, and teaching various aspects of ethics. Ethical behavior is obviously important for a fair and satisfactory functioning of individuals and groups. While much of it is common sense, much can be learned. Hopefully, this book will increase interest on this topic. More formal studies of collegiality are needed, and indeed, much is ongoing. The content of the book reflects the author's current view of collegiality and how it can be nurtured; it seems likely that others will have things they wish to add or perhaps things they disagree with. This is welcome; an ongoing conversation in this field can only be beneficial. Also, the book was written so that many could use it; it is written for the average person and requires no special expertise.

This book provides support for its statements and ideas. It relies on scientific studies where possible so that the presented ideas are justified. Scientific studies are not always interpreted correctly, nor do they always stand the test of time. But overall, they do give us at least some reason to believe what is said. Therefore, references to scientific studies and explanations are provided in many places. But it was not possible to be exhaustive and cite all of the work in a given area, so the references that are given should be considered examples of work in the area rather than comprehensive reviews of the topic. Backing up statements with evidence - evidence-based thinking - is an important skill not only for collegial ethics but also for our entire lives.

This book explains what collegial ethics is, its value, the impediments to it, and so forth. It is theoretical and didactic. As the writing progressed, it also became a self-help book in places. When any ethical topic such as collegial ethics is explained in concrete behavioral terms, and when guidelines and exercises are added, it becomes a self-help treatise, at least in part. This practical side is hopefully a strength of this book.

In addition to ethical guidelines, this book uses cases or stories as instruments for study and learning. By considering real-life situations exemplified through these cases, learning is both theoretical and practical, and one can see how the principles and tools of collegial ethics apply in day-to-day living. Cases are intended to reflect situations that might actually occur, and if you see yourself in a case, then this effort has been successful. But almost all cases in this book do not refer to any single, specific occurrence or person.

The book is an attempt at being a brief but complete discourse on collegiality. It is composed of three parts. The chapters in part I discuss collegial ethics, what it is, why we need it, and the tendencies in our psyches that can confuse us. A discussion of human nature and the role it plays in our interactions is one of the reasons this book is unique. Part II describes how we become collegial, the techniques we use, and the training we need to achieve this. It is the toolbox of collegial ethics. The chapters in part III discuss the limits of the topic and where we go from here. It also presents exercises for enhancing our requisite skills for collegiality. Although the settings for the cases in this book are mainly in academia and businesses, collegial ethics applies to all disciplines. An interesting exercise would be to examine if collegial ethics relates to some special issues or problems in your particular field of work.

As you read on, enjoy, and become a better and happier colleague and co-worker.

Notes for the Introduction

1. accessed on September 10, 2012, http://sourcesofinsight.com/help-your-colleagues-look-good/.

2. Kuhar, M. J. "Collegial Ethics: What, why and how." *Drug and Alcohol Dependence.* 119 (2011): 235–238..

3. Kuhar, M. J. Cross, D. "Collegial Ethics: Supporting Our Colleagues." *Science and Engineering Ethics* (April 26, 2012).

PART I

About Collegiality and Collegial Ethics, and Why Our Very Human Nature Underscores Its Need

1

Why Bother with Collegial Ethics?

*I know of no more encouraging fact than the unquestionable
ability of man to elevate his life by a conscious endeavor.*
—Henry David Thoreau [1]

What Is Collegial Ethics?

We use many kinds of ethics. For example, we have business ethics, situational ethics, medical ethics, etc. We also have books on spirituality, relationships, and good business practices. They undoubtedly help us, and this is why self-help books and books on personal development are so successful as a genre. The topic of this book, *collegial ethics, promotes supporting and being fair to our colleagues*, unless support is not appropriate or possible. It promotes supportive behavior even if the colleague is in trouble. [2,3] The word *ethics* is used because collegial ethics deals with the "principles of conduct governing an individual or group" which is the definition of ethics.[4] This word also hints of a moral imperative, something we need to do or take heed of. For many reasons, the time is right to address this topic. Actually it is overdue.

Most of us instinctively know what being supportive means. *Merriam-Webster*[4] defines *support* as: "to promote the interests or causes of, to uphold or defend as valid or correct, to argue or vote for, or assisting and helping." Note that in this definition there is no obvious or explicit gain for *us*. The focus is on helping *others*. But of course, if we all practice supportive behaviors, then we will also experience a personal gain. Our overall lives will be more enjoyable and productive, at least more often. Maybe sometimes our self-interest is really best served by promoting our collegial and mutual interests.

Sometimes being helpful is not easy, and we may not know what to do. Because of this, compassion and empathy, in addition to helping, have a high value in collegial ethics. If we can't act in an impactful and decisive way, then we can at least be empathetic and compassionate. These qualities also set us up to help others and provide us with the motivation to do so. Thus, collegial ethics is also defined as helping and having compassion and empathy for our colleagues. Sometimes, just being heard and seeing empathy and compassion in a friend is all the help that others need.

There are many failures in collegiality, and an important part of collegial ethics is exploring the basis for these failures. Sometimes they are due to our complex human nature and society. Understanding these so that we are not compelled to act out these failures is very, very important.

A Focus On Collegial Ethics Is Needed

Although general ethical training exists, a *focus* on collegial ethics is required to develop this needed field. Some might argue that this is just general ethics and no special attention to a collegial aspect is needed. But as noted above, we have subfields of ethics that include business ethics, situational ethics, medical ethics, etc. This is useful for providing an emphasis on the subfield and helps its development. Collegial (or coworker) ethics is no doubt as important as any other subfield, and perhaps it is even a foundation for some of them. It clearly deserves its own identity and special effort. In spite of the essential, constant and growing occurrence of collegial interactions, little or no formal training in collegial ethics is available. This is amazing. Fortunately, as noted above, many relevant skills have already been described elsewhere. Collegial ethics will include and emphasize many of these.

How Does It Work?

Supporting and being fair to our colleagues, which is the mandate of collegial ethics, can be done in hundreds of ways in various situations. Examples of this include giving someone a kind word after they suffer a loss, or just a nod indicating that you recognize a person and his or her problem, or even making suggestions. It could be as simple as listening to a tale of woe. It may involve physically helping someone who is injured or offering assistance to a colleague without being asked. Perhaps a young colleague who is not doing well is having trouble with his boss. You could help him by offering some of your time and expertise. You could say, "Hi, Al, can I help you? I'd be happy to meet with you and discuss the problem. Maybe I can make some suggestions that will be helpful to you." This kind of assistance can be greatly appreciated and earn you a lifelong friend.

More serious situations occur when someone is in trouble, and these may require more judgment, courage, and perhaps even restraint on your part. Consider a case where someone has been accused of inflating his or her expense accounts. If neither you nor anyone else seems to know what is true, these should be considered *alleged* accusations as far as you are concerned. If the opportunity seems right, you might say to the accused, "I'm sorry for your trouble." He or she may have plenty to say once the topic is addressed. It won't help to participate in gossipy speculations and hazy interpretations of the accused person's actions. Gossip or trash talking doesn't do anyone any good. A good rule is: first do no harm! Accusations and suspicions can be like a spreading disease that occupies everyone's thoughts and that hinders peaceful productivity.

The accusation could amount to nothing, since expenses can grow in some situations, such as being delayed while on travel because of storms or transportation failures. If the accusation proves to be true, then the person will be penalized, hopefully in a way that allows repentance and rehabilitation. Throughout this book many different scenarios will be presented and analyzed according to principles and guidelines of collegial ethics. How to be collegial will become clearer.

Isn't This Just Common Sense?

Why should we pay attention to collegial ethics? Isn't it just common sense? Often it *is* just common sense, but that doesn't mean that we will heed it. Voltaire said that common sense is not so common! Also, many common things are not easy to do and may require special efforts and skills. In spite of facing relatively simple problems, we are often so caught up in the minutia of surviving and being successful that we forget learned lessons in collegiality and we don't allow time to remember or improve these skills. We often allow our immediate and urgent problems to push aside our long term and strategic plans. Common sense isn't even allowed to be a factor.

Collegial Behavior Is Becoming Required

Collegial behavior is becoming more and more important in an interactive world. For example, collegiality is often a specific criterion for promotion. An example of this is given in Northern Illinois University's Statement on Professional Behavior of Employees: Collegiality Policy (Section II, Item 21). In this policy, collegiality is clearly stated as something that's highly desirable, and the policy has procedures to deal with "uncollegiality." Also, consider the following statement from the American Association of University Professors (AAUP):

In evaluating faculty members for promotion, renewal, tenure, and other purposes, American colleges and universities have customarily examined faculty performance in the three areas of teaching, scholarship, and service, with service sometimes divided further into public service and service to the college or university.... In recent years, Committee A has become aware of an increasing tendency...to add a fourth criterion in faculty evaluation: "collegiality."[5]

A recent book entitled *Collegiality and Service for Tenure and Beyond: Acquiring a Reputation as a Team Player* deals with this subject.[6] The first chapter is titled "Be Collegial or Perish." It is clear that collegiality is getting attention, and we need to deal with it even if we don't agree with it. Some seem to adapt very easily to this approach, but others resist or are unable to adapt because of habits or personal beliefs. Some colleagues, those who are selfish, insecure, awkward, or lack communication skills, may avoid collegial ethics. Ironically, they may be the ones who can benefit most from studying it. Some colleagues may even be anti-collegial, destructive or toxic in some cases. What do we do with them?

Younger faculty members in universities want collegiality. A survey carried out by the Harvard University Graduate School of Education that questioned forty-five hundred tenure-track faculty members at fifty-one colleges and universities revealed that tenure-track faculty members care more about collegiality and the culture of a department than they do about their workloads and compensation. Some said that the most important thing was to feel respected and valued in their jobs. This is a significant change over the results of earlier surveys, which reported that autonomy was the most important job factor—the ability and freedom to do and study what they wished. Collegiality, which has always been an important factor in our lives, is becoming more and more significant.[7]

Collegial ethics is a step in strengthening networking, which is often considered a significant career aid. After we make contact with other professionals, do we view them as competitors? In a sense, they are. What are the values we want to promote with our networked colleagues? Collegial ethics is a useful guide for this.

As the global economy becomes more widespread, as population densities increase, and as communications become even easier, we will be confronted with people-to-people interactions more frequently. Cell phones, Internet dating, and international chat rooms are clear evidence of this. Jeremy Rifkin, the author of a book on future economies titled *The Third Industrial Revolution*,[8] asserts that we are going to enter a new, collaborative era where relationships and empathetic engagements with others will have greater importance.

Collegiality Will Improve Our Lives and Institutions

Most of us mean well in our interactions with colleagues, but sometimes we are victims of dysfunctional aspects of our evolved human/animal nature and societal norms. Anti-collegiality can exist in many forms. Research has revealed that people who consistently demean their colleagues end up reducing the overall performance of their teams. Furthermore, negative interactions among colleagues can be very difficult to overcome. Bad interactions are more contagious, and they tend to outweigh good ones.[9]

It seems obvious that if we support our colleagues and live in a supportive culture where competition and debate are also appropriately honored, we will have a higher quality of life. A collegial atmosphere will improve collaborations and our own careers. Having support is important; we even live longer and healthier.[10, 11, 12] A focus on collegial ethics enhances our dignity and the democratic process. We become more aware of others' needs and look for a balanced and fair life that satisfies more people. Overall, it makes us stronger as a group.

Some of the most productive efforts in world history have required close cooperation among diverse kinds of colleagues. Think of the development of nuclear power or going to the moon. Although there are many successes, one wonders how many complex projects have failed because of dysfunction in the groups. Collegial ethics not only has value in that it will improve our environments, it also means that people will be more productive.

Collegial Ethics Will Counterbalance "Accusative" Ethics

Much existing ethical training, at least in graduate schools, focuses on finding errors, fraud, faults, and failures in others, and on how to be a whistle blower. This can set a tone of suspicion, caution, and promote isolation in a work setting. Sometimes we end up looking over our shoulders, hoping that a routine behavior is not viewed as suspicious or inappropriate.

For example, consider this case. Student X was writing down numbers as they appeared on a computer screen. The numbers were data from a certain experiment. It turns out that he wasn't writing down the exact numbers, but rather numbers that were a little different from those on the monitor. Student Z, who recently took a course in research misconduct and was nearby, noticed the difference in the numbers and became suspicious. He mentioned it to other students and the department chairperson, and before long, there was a persistent rumor that Student X was "making up data". Before Student X even realized it, his colleagues and superiors were viewing him with suspicion, and he was even shunned by his friends. When confronted by his very stern department chairperson, he was able to readily explain what was going on. When writing down the numbers that appeared on the monitor, Student X was subtracting out a small background value in his head, something that the computer wasn't doing for him, and then writing down the difference. The value had to be subtracted to process the data further, and the original data was stored in the computer so nothing was lost. There was nothing inappropriate going on, except that an observer saw something, judged it erroneously, and shared it inappropriately. Instead of describing what he *saw* and separating that from his own *interpretation* of it, Student Z just blabbed nonsense without ever asking what was happening. Moreover, he thought it was his *duty* to report it (or what he thought it was).

Collegial ethics, which focuses on support and respect of our colleagues, is needed as a positive counterbalance to this accusative tendency. Student Z could have discreetly approached Student X or the chairperson before communicating his fantasies to others. Instead, he immediately thought of wrongdoing and started gossip.

We Harvest More When We Tend and Nourish Our Garden

The analogy of tending a garden applies here. We can't survive by only taking food from the garden. We must also plant, cultivate, and fertilize it. In fact, we need to perform these tasks before we can enjoy even the smallest benefit of a garden. Gardening requires delaying our reward or gratification because planting and nurturing does not bring an immediate reward, but rather a reward some months in the future. Additional knowledge and study may be needed as well. For example, some lands and climates are better suited to certain crops. In collegial ethics, we must first get training in specific skills before we can use them and help others. In the same way that planting and nurturing is as important as reaping our harvests, developing our collegial skills is just as important as the act of helping others (and ourselves). Other sections in this book focus on how to develop collegial skills.

A Nightmare Scenario

As noted above, there are many possible situations where collegial ethics apply - from the smallest interaction with an upset colleague, to truly serious situations that impact peoples' lives for a long time. It's the truly serious and difficult situations that most obviously need collegial attention. Minor problems would include a small traffic accident or a blow up with the boss. But situations can arise where someone has been significantly hurt in some way and needs support. Consider the following case.

You discover certain practices in your group and maybe elsewhere that are clearly unethical, and you complain to people in charge. As a result, many powerful people feel threatened, and someone loses his or her job. People become frightened, self protective and start pointing fingers – and guess what – you get blacklisted for your actions even though you were only trying to stop unethical behavior.

(Blacklisting indicates that your existence is tolerated but that you are treated poorly and denied typical opportunities. It is put in place by a group or individual, and others are required to participate and enforce it, or be blacklisted themselves. It lasts as long as the initiating blacklisters say it lasts – which could be forever. It could be put in place even for a trivial reason).

You are respected in your field and doing very well. Nevertheless, the blacklisting slowly takes effect, and your career is blunted. You are demonized by the blacklisters who are afraid for themselves, and your reputation is seriously damaged. While some claim to offer solutions, in reality, their help is too little and too late, and there is very little you can do to rectify the situation. The colleagues who attempt to help you are worried that they might be blacklisted themselves and they soon give up trying to help because they are afraid. Some even join the transgressors and conspire against you behind your back. Even though you have been denied due process by the blacklisters, and the blacklisting exceeds the nature of your so-called "crime, (in this case there never was one)" you are nevertheless a victim who is suffering the retribution of being a whistleblower. Reports from many other whistleblowers[13, 14] reveal that many suffer retribution, and, in general, do not do well in their careers after whistleblowing. The reasons for this are complex and presumably involve the more twisted and puzzling aspects of human nature. Personalities are varied, extend from the generous to the sociopathic, and some of the blacklisters even seem to enjoy their role. You find yourself in a nightmare.

Blacklisting, which is practiced in some groups, includes several serious ethical failures. It's a failure to engage in "due process" which would allow a fair clarification about what happened and a clear determination if a punishment is needed. The punishment must fit the crime. Also, blacklisting is a process where others are forced to participate. The ethics of bullying applies to blacklisters and that is discussed in chapter 3. Also, we are pressed to abdicate our right to decide for ourselves how justice is served and who is guilty. We allow a small group or individual to decide it for us; it's a failure of taking responsibility for our own actions. It can also be a *failure of courage* because of fear. It is said that "sometimes blacklisting is the only way" to get justice; that may be true *sometimes*, but is it worth forgetting about basic human rights such as due process and having a punishment that fits the nature of the crime (if there is one)? Those can't be forgotten. What do we do with the blacklisters, many of whom seem to be without conscience? What about their arrogance where they play god? Blacklisting is dangerous, denigrates everyone involved, and is most often unethical. It needs to be challenged by courageous, clear thinking and responsible individuals.

As a victim, what can you do in this particularly bleak situation? What would be a good survival strategy? You may find that you are very stressed and are not making good decisions. In general, you need to find help. Hopefully, you will be able to find some believers in collegial ethics who also have sufficient courage to help. As a victim, you need to find ways to maintain your self-esteem, keep supportive colleagues, and continue professional productivity. You need to persist in fighting the situation so that you can regain control of your life. There are also professionals, who are trained to deal with this type of stress and its victims, and some useful suggestions for victims have been published.[13] Strong and effective protection for whistleblowers continues to be a challenging problem and needs to be addressed further. What could you or others do if you developed the kind of paralyzing fear described in Chapter 2?

Someone in this position is likely to see the value of collegial ethics. Very difficult cases like this need to be studied and discussed in collegial groups. Principles and strategies need to be posed and tested.

Do We Have To Give Up Competition?

What about competition? We're all competing, and aren't we supposed to compete? Competitiveness is embedded, promoted, and essential for successful businesses and careers. Competitiveness is believed to be a requirement for success in a free-market system. An issue here is whether it could be viewed as the antithesis of collegiality. It is not. Competitiveness and collegiality can coexist. They must. Competition is a good thing, but it is not the only good thing. Can competitiveness get out of hand? Of course it can. Collegial ethics is needed in competitive situations because it will be a positive counterbalance for forces that tend to push people apart. It promotes the skills that make it easier for competitors to work together. How do we find the proper balance among self interest, competition, debate, and collegiality? This is discussed further in chapter 7 in a section on self-interest and where there is a case about friends wanting help with a competitive final exam. The balance among competition, debate, and collegiality is a fruitful topic for discussion in this field.

Successful Precedents

Many precedents demonstrate that collegial ethics has been and will continue to be effective. Many individuals have assembled themselves in formal groups for mutual support and advancement. For example, American Women in Science have grouped together and focus on issues of common concern. A psychologist from Colorado began a colleague assistance program after he needed help with a problem in his counseling practice.[15] Other groups as diverse as school administrators, faculty, and dentists have also looked for collegial support.[2]

As mentioned above, some feel that by ourselves we can't really make a difference and wonder why we should bother trying. To respond to this question, we can remember the story of a child walking along the beach, returning stranded starfish to the sea. He patiently picked up each one and waded into the surf, dropping them into the water. An adult, who was somewhat of a skeptic, said to the child, "Why are you doing that? There are so many starfish on this beach that you can't really make any difference." But the child looked up just as he dropped one in the water and said, "But I made a difference for *that* one."[16] We can catalog our successes, one small one at a time.

The Bottom Line

Collegial ethics promotes a set of guidelines on how to help colleagues in everyday situations. These situations could be of minor impact, or they could fall in the category of a nightmare experience. There are many reasons to incorporate collegial ethics into our lives; certainly it will make everyone's life better. The value of collegiality is growing in our society and is going to be more important in the future. It does not mean that we will have to give up competition and debate, only that we will have to think of others' needs as well. There are many successful precedents where colleagues have grouped together to help each other. It clearly can be done.

Notes for Chapter 1

1. "Quotes on Self Improvement," accessed on July 9 2012, http://www.quotationcollection.com/tag/self%20improvement/quotes,.

2. Kuhar, M. J. "Collegial Ethics: What, why and how," *Drug and Alcohol Dependence* (2011) 119:235–238.

3. Kuhar, M. J., Cross, D. "Collegial Ethics: Supporting Our Colleagues," *Sci Eng Ethics*. (April 26, 2012). Published online on April 26. See also http://www.springerlink.com/content/w211mj45511445k6/fulltext.pdf

4. *Merriam-Webster's Collegiate Dictionary*. Tenth Edition. (Springfield:Merriam-Webster Inc. 1999.)

5. "On Collegiality as a Criterion for Faculty Evaluation," AAUP, accessed on March 22, 2012, http://www.aaup.org/AAUP/pubsres/policydocs/contents/collegiality.htm.

6. Silverman, F. H. *Collegiality and Service for Tenure and Beyond*. (Westport: Praeger Publishers, 2004.)

7. Fogg, P. "Young PhDs Say Collegiality Matters More Than Salary." *The Chronicle of Higher Education* 53(6): A1 (2006): A1, 2, or view at http://chronicle.com/article/Young-PhDs-Say-Collegiality/4178/

8. Rifkin, J. *The Third Industrial Revolution*. (Palgrave McMillan: New York, 2011.)

9. Gillespie, B. B. "No Jerks: Some Firms Argue That Collegiality Pays Off," *ABA Journal*, (March 1 issue), accessed on March 22, 2012, http://www.abajournal.com/magazine/article/no_jerks_some_firms_argue_that_collegiality_pays.

10. Mirowsky J., Catherine E. Ross. "Family Relationships, Social Support, and Subjective Life Expectancy," *Journal of Health and Social Behavior*, 43 (2002) 4469–489.

11. Antonucci, TC, KS Cortina, and KL Fiori. "Social Network Typologies and Mental Health Among Older Adults," *The Journals of Gerontology Series B: Psychological Sciences and Social Sciences* 61B, no. 1 (2006): 25–32.

12. Okabayashi, H., et al., "Mental Health among Older Adults in Japan: Do Sources of Social Support and Negative Interaction Make a Difference?" *Social Science & Medicine* 59, no. 11 (2004): 2259–2270.

13. Alford, F. C. *Whistleblowers: Broken Lives and Organizational Power*. (Ithica: Cornell University Press, 2001).

14. Joy, A. B. *Whistleblower*. (Point Richmond: Bay Tree Publishing, 2010).

15. Munsey, C. "Helping Colleagues to Help Themselves," *Monitor* no. 37 (2006): 35.

16. Adapted from Eisley, L. *The Star Thrower*. (New York: Harvest Books, 1978).

2

Games We Play With Ourselves

We are all capable of believing things which we know to be untrue, and then, when we are finally proved wrong, impudently twisting the facts so as to show that we were right.
—George Orwell[1]

We often hear, "We're all busy. Stopping to chat and offering to help others seems like a waste of time. I don't think anybody wants it. What good would it do anyway? We don't have any problems around here."

Are these statements true? Or are they excuses, just sayings that convince people that they don't have to get involved with colleagues? Not getting involved is certainly less bother. Is avoiding bother the real reason they don't get involved? The bulk of this chapter is about why we don't always support other people. There are many reasons, but one of them is that we can easily *convince ourselves* that there are good reasons for not getting involved. Although there can be much truth in these self-convincing rationales, we can also distort situations in our minds so that we can justify inaction. By generating these distortions, we feel safer and more comfortable in avoiding the issues. The real reasons that we behave this way are undoubtedly complex, involving the protective reflexes in our brains that evolved over eons and that kept us safe in our ancestral past. It is worth bringing these processes to light so that we are more aware of them, which is the first step in trying to be free of them and to have greater freedom in our choices.

Keep The Peace

Many collegial problems are brushed under the conference table because we don't want to deal with them. We want to *keep the peace*, which is a noble idea, and an important value to some. A peaceful job environment is very nice. But in reality, it could be that keeping the peace means that you are ignoring a problem that will fester. An offended or insulted colleague may feel guilty about making a fuss and therefore remain quiet - until it overwhelms him. Because small problems often blow over and are forgotten, trying to keep the peace seems like a good idea. But it can easily leave disgruntled folks behind.

Given how desirable a peaceful environment can be, we sometimes choose to impose the peace by decree without addressing the issues. But this can backfire and cause bigger problems later. One supervisor did not ignore the problem and dealt with disruption directly and effectively in the following case. The supervisor was in charge of eight people who had various sequential tasks to perform. If one person did not function, then that slowed down the overall process. It turned out that Person A started dating Person B's significant other, and Person B felt betrayed and angry. Many of the others in the groups sided with B and were angry with A. The hostility grew, and the group became dysfunctional. Individuals walked out of the work area, there was open hostility among them, and both A and B started taking sick days.

The supervisor tried to order everyone to get back to work, but that really didn't work. So she thought about it and decided on a strategy. She met with each person in the group, exhibited compassion and empathy, and collected a list of gripes. Sometimes she scheduled repeat meetings. Most of the issues had to do with Person

B's betrayal, but there were some additional issues as well. Just by listening, the supervisor seemed to calm the group down, but there was still turmoil. She called the group together and laid out the complaints. She said she understood because she was a human being like everyone else. Some of the complaints she dealt with by making changes in work assignments, but others were not in the jurisdiction of the workplace. For example, dating habits were not things that she should get involved with, and she said so. She was very firm in stating that personal problems, even though important, should not be brought into the workplace. They could be discussed at lunch, on break, or after work, but not during work hours. People who were not doing their jobs, for whatever reason, would have to solve their problems and improve their performances. She said that she respected everyone's personal lives and wanted everyone to do well and be happy, but in the end she was responsible for productivity. She was willing to take the time to work with the group to restore harmony and to counsel people, but stated that everyone had to get back to work. She asked that everyone avoid discussing the situation between A and B. She acknowledged that it was important to them, but it was not part of the job and should be dealt with off the job site. Gradually, normal work resumed.

In this case, the peace was effectively restored because the situation was analyzed and dealt with. Problems that are not dealt with can fester and seethe to the point that the problem becomes amplified. In those cases, keeping the peace as a sacred goal could be counterproductive. More will be said about this later when we talk about conflict resolution.

What I Do Won't Matter

"What I do or say or think won't matter. Why should I try to be nice to others or build collegial relationships when nobody will care?" This can simply be an excuse for laziness or a fear that we don't quite have the social skills we need to be collegial. It also could be a veiled angry response based on past disappointments such as collegial rejections and a lack of interest and help; so someone may not get involved because they didn't receive what he or she needed in the past. It could also be a response from a sarcastic or defeated person, who may really believe that his or her response won't matter. In these cases where neglect and misfortune have soured people, the decision to avoid involvement could be a perpetuation of that neglect. Mentoring to achieve successes would be helpful here. We don't always think so, but we really can have an impact on others and on our environments by judicious and effective actions.

Let Them Do It Themselves

"Let them do it themselves" is something we often hear or think when considering helping another. Doing it themselves emphasizes self reliance, and very often doing it themselves is the most efficient and effective way to get something done, particularly if we have the needed skills. But sometimes, maybe more often than we think, we can't do it ourselves; we need help. Let them do it themselves is often one of our myths and self deceptions.

Let's go back to our early life. As a newborn, we wouldn't live more than a few hours without mother's nourishing milk. The need for support carries on throughout our early life, and it is clear that we humans have a longer period of dependence than many other animals. We need socializing, schools, doctors, and mentoring. The need for support is reduced as we grow older and we then begin to offer others support. But our need for support and help from others doesn't really end.

If we want to have children, we need a spouse. If we want food for sustenance, we need a grocer. If we want to learn something, we need a teacher or a school. If we are sick, we need a doctor. If we are wronged, we need the law. If we are wronged and want to address it, we need witnesses to come forward. If we want to work, we need an employer or someone to buy our products. If we want to build shelter, we need a builder or supplier of materials. If we want to express our spirituality, we need a pastor and a church. If we want to experience love, intimacy, and compassion, we need a close friend or partner. And on and on it goes. When it comes to many things that really matter, we need someone else. Saying "Let them do it themselves" can be a serious self deception.

Self-Righteous Judgment

When we hear of a colleague who needs help, we sometimes respond with a self-righteous judgment. We often say, "I'll take care of myself, and he can take care of himself." or, "She deserves it." and, "He got himself into it; let him get himself out of it." This kind of attitude is an armor that blocks compassion and involvement.

Jonathan Haidt, a moral psychologist, sees righteousness as an evolved and useful behavior that keeps us together in communities, and communities are one of the reasons humans are so successful in surviving and advancing. The idea is that righteousness exists because it is beneficial to both us and our communities. It's a kind of bonding mechanism. However, he points out that although righteousness gives us community, heroism, altruism, and sainthood, it also gives us war, genocide, and conflicting politics.[2] There is always another side of the coin, so to speak. Which side we use depends on the situation, our experiences, our judgment, and our ideals. Collegiality should be at least one of the major values that we consider in every situation.

There is also the kind of righteous blame that is rooted in guilt and shame. Sometimes, when we hear about others' misfortunes, our reaction is shame or even guilt. We feel shame or guilt because we are ok and they are not. But, we can banish that feeling of shame or guilt by finding a way to blame that person for his or her problem. In doing that, we don't have to spend energy on shame and compassion or in acting to help. Blocking out these feelings with righteousness and blame of others works, in a sense.

Blaming others might be justified in some situations; sometimes people do risky things like walking down a dark alley at night in a very bad neighborhood. If something bad happens to them, we can blame their poor judgment. In other situations, poor judgment may not have caused their misfortunes. Even if they have used poor judgment, reacting with compassion is collegial. Sometimes we shun people in trouble, and shunning them, which can be inhumane, compounds the problem.

Excessive Fairness

Excessive fairness is subtle, but common, and can have a significant effect. Even though it may be clear that a colleague is not being treated fairly and needs help, a person may avoid speaking up to help that colleague by convincing him- or herself that there is another side to the story, and because he or she *wants to be fair,* they don't do anything. If you are searching for the other side of the story "to be fair", even though you know the other side can't be justified, you can avoid or delay being supportive. We might actually convince ourselves that it is a superior position. After all, what's better than fairness? To be *fair,* we might say, "Well, she must have done something to get that kind of treatment," which isn't necessarily true. Or, in trying to be fair, you might express positive opinions to both parties involved, which can compound the problem because then both sides feel like they are in the right (the "false consensus" phenomenon).[3] We can find many ways to avoid acting on an issue.

Questionable Wisdom

We often think that helping others can get us into trouble - sometimes with good reason - so, we think it's smart to avoid involvement. One might say, "My daddy didn't raise a fool." or, "I can't endanger my family's future." There is obviously some truth in these comments, and it's essential to be careful and thoughtful about getting involved in a situation. But even in the face of trouble, it might be best to get involved. Avoiding trouble might only create more trouble in the future, and avoiding action now because of family safety, for example, might only degrade your family's future security. It all depends on the situation and what's at stake for us.

One remedy for this kind of thinking is to consider the *positive* things that will happen if we get involved and become active. Focus on the good things that will follow from our actions. How many people will benefit and in what ways? Will it improve our personal reputation in the eyes of others? How many favorable forecasts can you imagine?

Another problem is that there are many who would categorize some supportive colleagues disparagingly as "do-gooders." Many believe that do-gooders can only get in trouble, and they may even have contempt for them. Actual studies suggest that so-called do-gooders, in their unselfishness, can create discomfort. They are often disliked by coworkers, paradoxically, for selfish reasons. Because do-gooders increase expectations of everyone else, and because their generous behavior will make others look bad, they are often disliked. Colleagues can even complain that do-gooders have ulterior and selfish motives for being generous.[4] How do we handle "do-gooders" in our environments? Can we and/or they make adjustments so that we feel more compatible and comfortable with them?

Giving Disliking Too Much Influence

It seems fairly common to allow a *dislike* of someone to influence our actions. "I just don't like him; therefore, I won't get involved with him." *But* liking and disliking should *not* be a major factor when functioning in the professional world, although practically speaking, it does play a role. Sometimes people feel that they need to follow their *feelings*. We hear that a lot. Being able to say, "I felt that..." is a way of justifying your actions. However, although feelings are important factors in very personal relationships and friendships, they are not important factors in professional relationships. *Appropriate behavior* and a focus on achieving common goals is more important (just ask your boss) than liking the people we work with, although liking them might make it easier. Inappropriately expressing your dislike for a colleague could easily have a negative effect. Focusing on liking, disliking, and emotional feelings instead of professional goals can be counterproductive.

Suppose you are working in a group to organize a major event. Your leader says you should team up with Person M because both of you have expertise to get a certain task done. But you really dislike Person M. You don't like M's looks and her mannerisms really get on your nerves. While groaning to a friend, you make the mistake of saying you really can't stand M. Unfortunately, M either overhears you or finds out about your comment, and then she makes a mistake by confronting you and telling you that you aren't so wonderful, nobody likes you, and that you don't have anything to offer the project. The lack of wisdom continues and you storm out. On the way, you say to your leader that you just can't work with M and call her some unpleasant names. Others see this, become upset, and are distracted from their work. They take sides and spend time debating the issue. The team leader is a little shocked and worries about the best way to get back on track. Should both M and you be fired or replaced? Replacing you and M could be a good solution because then each of you would be happy (not really?), the leader won't have to worry about future blowups, and the group can get back to work. When you hear about this possibility, you aren't happy because the group project was very important to you, and it looked like a way to get ahead. The cycle will continue unless you and M begin to act in a way that allows the group to move ahead. It would have helped if you hadn't made a comment about M in the first place. M could have been more mature and realized that your disliking of her was unimportant — yes, unimportant - given the job at hand. M also could have said that she wanted to be liked, but the job at hand required you to work together and nothing more. The entire event and your leader's loss of confidence in you and M could have been avoided. It is unfortunate that dislike can be the reason for a group's failure. Obviously, simple *dislike of a person can never justify destructive actions* toward that person.

More can be said about expressing feelings. Sometimes it can't be stopped. Maybe people haven't worked at controlling emotions enough. Or maybe the feelings are so strong that they can't be controlled. Hopefully the feelings and emotions won't be too destructive. Sometimes including our feelings in our communications can be very powerful and useful. It can be productive to express certain feelings in certain ways. This is described in chapter 6.

Genuine Paralyzing Fear

We find some situations so threatening that we experience a paralyzing fear. This is neither a game nor a self-deception; it's a real physiologic paralysis. It may be rooted in a survival response that's hardwired into the brain. When a situation is inescapable or threatening, we freeze in indecision; one could argue that this is positive because it theoretically gives us time to think about an escape. Or perhaps we freeze so that a predator has difficulty in seeing us. Other similar responses seem hardwired into our behavior. For example, a sudden intense stimulus, such as a loud noise, creates a response of fear, alertness, and a desire to move away from the noise. Another stimulus is novelty; we are afraid of the unknown. For example, infants show fear of strangers. Fear is one of the basic emotions that psychologists have been studying for decades, and we know a fair amount about it. We have learned the hormonal responses to it and the parts of the body and brain that mediate it.[5,6,7] It is very important for survival but can also be pathological, excessive, and crippling. Post-traumatic stress disorder (PTSD), commonly found in war veterans, is considered a pathological, debilitating, and excessively fearful reaction to some triggers, such as a loud noise. While fear may sometimes debilitate us, it often can be treated and managed successfully.

What do we do if we find ourselves frozen in fear and are just not able to carry on as we should? This could happen in many ways. It could prevent an injured person from seeking redress, or it could prevent someone from protective actions when they are threatened. It could prevent you from coming to someone's aid. This kind of fear/shock/trauma freezing reaction to a situation is really debilitating. If it is important to overcome our fear in a situation, we may need help, perhaps professional help.

The Bottom Line

There are many ways to avoid helping others, and they can sometimes involve self-deceptions. Although there is some validity to these responses, they can be used excessively and are distortions of danger and logic. Righteousness, excessive fairness, questionable wisdom, and disliking others *are simply patterns and responses rather than compelling realities.* Being aware of our ability to distort reality gives us perspective and an awareness of other responses, possibly more constructive ones. Focusing on the positive outcomes of our actions can be a powerful antidote to those feelings and provide a more complete picture of the situation.

Notes for Chapter 2

1. "George Orwell Quotes," Goodreads, accessed on July 12, 2012, http://www.goodreads.com/author/quotes/3706.George_Orwell.

2. Haidt, J. "Why We Need to Be Righteous." *New Scientist* 213 no 2854 (2012): 30–31.

3. Greene, D., P. House, and L. Ross, "The False Consensus Effect," *Experimental Social Psychology* 13 (1977): 279–301.

4. Sorenson E. "People don't really like unselfish colleagues," *WSU News* accessed on April 24, 2012, http://wsutoday.wsu.edu/pages/publications.asp?Action=Detail&PublicationID=21047.

5. Davis, M. and K. M. Myers. "Mechanisms of Fear Extinction," *Mol Psychiatry* 2, Review. PMID: 17160066 (February 12, 2007):120–50.

6. Davis M. "Neurobiology of Fear Responses: the Role of the Amygdala," *Journal of Neuropsychiatry & Clinical Neurosciences*, 9(3) Review. PMID: 9276841 (Summer 1997): 382–402.

7. Davis, M. "Pharmacological and Anatomical Analysis of Fear Conditioning," *NIDA Research Monographs* 97 Review. PMID: 2247135 (1990):126–62.

3

Human Nature, Evolved Instincts and Culture—Can We Change?

The next step in mans evolution will be the survival of the wisest. —Deepak Chopra[1]

To change the world, start with yourself.—Anonymous[2]

Evolved? You mean like evolution? Well, yes, that's the idea. Evolution is a hot-button topic for many; however it is critical for understanding what it means to be a human being. Evolution is a *theory*, but the word *theory* is used in the scientific sense, where it's much more than just an idea.[3, 4] The evidence for evolution is overwhelming, even if you leave out fossils. Many would say that this is very good because continuing evolution provides humans with a mechanism for continuing adaptation and survival in spite of difficult future challenges. Evolution has produced our human nature and understanding human nature and why and how we react to our world is a foremost problem of our time. Understanding human nature ultimately requires us to understand the brain which is the organ of behavior, and it has clearly evolved over time.[5, 6]

One way to look at the brain is to think of it as grandma's attic. When we get there, we find many fascinating things; some are old and some are new. Some are recognizable and familiar, and some are a little strange and puzzling. We don't know how some things got there or what they were used for. But they are there nevertheless and they did come from somewhere, and presumably had a purpose at some point. They might be helpful and useful in the current world, or they might not. This chapter is about the things we don't easily recognize and about their possible functions and uses. The brain promotes many behaviors that are rooted in the past, that were important at some point for our survival perhaps, but don't obviously fit into the current world. They are the mysteries in grandma's attic. If we pay attention to these mysteries and behaviors, we can probably learn something about ourselves. Some of these behaviors might be collegial, but some might not be.

This chapter, like the last one, examines factors that impact on our ability to support others. If we are unaware of these perhaps subconscious factors, they may influence our behavior in ways we don't necessarily want. But if we are aware of them, we can operate more freely and fully. This also provides a strong rationale for training, as you will see. Focusing on collegial ethics, which proposes supporting our colleagues, is needed to overcome the biases that we knowingly—or unknowingly—carry.

Many of our actions and reactions are *automatic*. We drive to work without really thinking about the route we take, we automatically respond to colleagues with a "good morning" greeting, and we instinctively open our arms to our children. Why is this so? Is the human brain wired to react in certain ways? If it is wiring instead of the influence of culture, is it because our behaviors (and our brains) have evolved and provide an economy of energy and a survival advantage? Would we be lost or hurt without these reflexive behaviors? Evolution is complex, but yes, many would say that our responses provide a survival advantage, or at least they did at some point in our ancestral past. Because our actions are so critical to our well-being, it is essential that we understand their underlying causes and roots. Can our automatic responses be disadvantageous? If so, when? We can't fully answer these questions yet, but we have some of the answers.

Many, though probably not all of our automatic emotions are innate and products of evolution. Various other species exhibit innate responses, so why shouldn't we? Available evidence says that at least some of our responses are instinctual. Darwin noted this in his book *Emotions in Man and Animals*,[7] published in 1872. Being an astute observer and good thinker, he had good reasons for this idea. He was able to rule out cultural influences on some emotional expressions by observing that emotions appear in young children who have not yet had an opportunity for cultural learning. Many emotional expressions, such as crying and smiling, are found across different human cultures, and even people who are born blind mimic the emotional expressions of others who are not similarly deprived. Darwin further pointed out that nonhuman animals also produce similar emotional expressions. Thus, the idea that emotional responses are at least partially innate has a long history and has been supported many times.

What does this have to do with collegial ethics? We often avoid supporting or helping people for reasons that we don't totally understand. This was touched upon in the last chapter. Our responses seem to be almost automatic, and we presumably need to look at evolution (and sometimes cultural differences) to explain these reactions. Certain instincts or quick responses provided a survival advantage in ancestral environments and were selected for during evolution, as Darwin pointed out. For example, we instinctively avoid those who are ill because we might catch a disease. We instinctively avoid those with odd or aggressive behaviors because they may be dangerous. We avoid those who are different because we don't know what to expect, and we therefore aren't comfortable with them. These instincts and reactions have evolved in our psyche over millions of years.[8-12] Moreover, our evolved instincts err on the side of safety.

In other words, we react to avoid dangers even though the chance of a real danger may be low. This is sort of like a smoke detector that goes off when there is smoke from cooking. We'd prefer this overly sensitive response rather than one that might miss a real threat. But a point is that these reflexes, which keep us from helping and getting involved with others in certain circumstances, can also prevent us from the benefits those people can offer us. Helping an injured person can help that person return to an active and productive role in society. Also, wouldn't we want help if we were in that situation?

The problem with these automatic responses is well-known. Although they have been important for our survival over many generations, they do not *always* serve us well in the modern world. For example, the ill and handicapped can be cured or treated and may have much to offer us if we don't turn away from them too quickly. Those in nursing and other helping professions, through training, overcome any avoidance issues they might experience. Moreover, our automatic responses can endanger us or put us in a bad light. Imagine someone who ran from a mugging but then realized that he or she could have helped the victim by screaming or calling the police. Carl Sagan and E. O. Wilson commented on this irony by stating that we have created a civilization that is startlingly advanced, but yet we have Paleolithic emotions and medieval institutions.[13]

It is certainly easy to avoid colleagues who are suffering some kind of failure, such as losing their jobs or causing an accident where someone was hurt. But if we grow to understand that this avoidance reaction is only a reflex, and not a mandatory response, and if we train ourselves to overcome those reactions when we choose to, we might act differently. We might very well have the courage and confidence, born of training and practice, to offer our colleagues a word of understanding and compassion. Training, discussion, and practice make a big difference. Sometimes the seemingly impossible becomes possible. Simply showing compassion can make a difference in others' lives. After seeing an unfortunate person, English preacher

John Bradford said, "There but for the grace of God go I." We know what it means to feel compassion.

These are not the only situations where we need to be aware of innate and automatic responses. The same is true in making decisions about our friendships, futures, and especially our lives. Understanding our evolution-based and innate responses is a *problem of fundamental importance*. Only when we truly understand ourselves and our tendencies—many of which appear irrational and overly protective—can we form a realistic plan for society and our future.

Obedience To Authority: The Shocking Work Of Stanley Milgram

Authorities tell us to do many things throughout our lives. Respecting authority is a mark of a good citizen and a mature person. But does authority have its limits? How do we look at authority?

In the early 1960s, Dr. Stanley Milgram at Yale carried out a series of experiments that revealed how willing we are to obey authority, even though we are causing serious distress to others.[14-16] Dr. Milgram looked the perfect image of a serious, knowledgeable and authoritative scientist in a lab coat that recruited subjects to act as "teachers", who would administer shocks to "students" when they failed to learn a word pair. The naïve recruit acting as a "teacher" was told that this was an experiment to study the effects of punishment on learning. The shock apparatus was designed so that shocks of increasing severity could be given if the "student" kept giving wrong answers. The student, actually a colleague of Dfr. Milgram's who was secretly told what to do, was strapped into a chair and an electrode was attached to his wrist to deliver the shocks. When the student gave a wrong answer, Dr. Milgram, in the room with the teacher, told the teacher to deliver a shock. As the student kept giving wrong answers, the teacher was instructed to give shocks of greater and greater intensity. Soon the student began to complain about the shocks. At higher intensities of electrical shock, the student began to cry out, even scream, and demanded to be released from the experiment. The "teacher" who was pushing the button to deliver the shocks could hear the complaints and even showed distress when delivering the shock.

Even though the "student" appeared to be in serious distress, he really *wasn't* getting any shock at all. He was only pretending to be shocked, and he had been trained to act this way by Dr. Milgram. But the teacher really did think he/she was shocking the student. Dr. Milgram sternly insisted that the shocks be delivered. He also repeatedly insisted that the intensity be increased when multiple errors were made even though the student appeared seriously stressed and outraged at being shocked in a chair that he was strapped to. The students were good actors.

So what did the "teachers" do? How did they respond? Did they follow the directions of authority who was Dr. Milgram? How did they deal with their conscience when they appeared to be shocking a harmless and distressed person who was basically helpless? Well, the results are upsetting and surprising to many. Sixty two percent of the "teachers" continued to shock the vocally complaining "students" under the insistence of Dr. Milgram, the authority figure in the room. This is roughly 6 out of 10 who were obedient in spite of their role in creating serious distress for another who wasn't threatening in any way. The results were about the same whether the teachers were either men or women, and the results found by Milgram were repeated and confirmed in many other laboratories. This is a believable result about human nature.

Certain conditions of the experiment were varied to explore this tendency further. When the teacher did not have to press the shock button himself because he was able to instruct another to do it, 92% obeyed. More obeyed when they were one step removed from delivering the shock.

When the person in charge (Dr. Milgram) appeared as an ordinary person rather than an authoritative figure in a lab coat, the percentage of those who obeyed dropped from 62 to about 20 %. The perception of real authority, or looking like an authority, was important for obedience. If the authority figure was not in the room but instructed the teacher from another room, there was a similar drop in obedience to about 20%. So the authority figure had to be more present to fully exert the authority.

What about those who did not fully obey - the 4 out of the 10? One was more educated than the others and presumably viewed the authority figure as a peer rather than as an overriding authority. He had the confidence needed to disobey. It has been suggested that education is a positive factor in judging the validity of the commands of authority.

How do we analyze this? Do people want to inflict pain on others? Probably not. One idea is that the obedient person *adjusts his view of him or herself* such that they do not feel in charge or responsible for the shocking; the authority figure in charge is responsible; they just push the button. Does this suggest that the obedient person is more vulnerable to doing hurtful acts? Perhaps yes. Obedience can be passive, while the person who disobeys must have the gumption to disobey or act differently. This may require some courage, which is a significant issue in collegial ethics and courage is discussed further elsewhere in this book.

How does this affect us? We certainly aren't going to allow ourselves to be strapped into a chair and shocked. But perhaps we need to think about the proper role and ethics of obedience. Maybe we need to ask: "Are there situations where we should disobey – or at least question?" Perhaps the obedient ones need to think about the impact of obedient actions on themselves and others. Obedience can certainly be advantageous if the authorities have experience and our best interest at heart. They can save us from making mistakes.

But in the light of Milgram's experiments, there may be situations, probably rare, where we need to at least raise issues with authority. If you see a colleague in a situation where obedience is having a negative impact, you can very reasonably ask yourself if the obedience is appropriate. Similarly, authorities have to respect their authority lest they abuse it. Milgram showed that many people are simply obedient and could cause distress to others when told to do so. The discovery of this aspect of human nature places a greater burden on authorities to use their power wisely.

This willingness to obey may be at the foundation of the phrase: "I was always taught…" That phrase is often used to justify an opinion or action. Can we question what we were taught?

Our Emotions and Control

How we think, behave, and arrive at conclusions has been studied. Consider the following story from Jonathan Haidt's book, *The Happiness Hypothesis*.[17] This story illustrates the complexity of what happens in our minds when we are suddenly very frightened. Think of an elephant with a rider who is guiding the elephant to move timber, which is their job. The rider is very skilled and gets the strong elephant to do a great deal of work, and they are a superb team. Now, what happens when a lion or tiger springs from the bushes and attacks them? We wouldn't be surprised if the elephant becomes frightened, rears up, and runs away, trampling anything in its path. The elephant runs perhaps because its parents taught it to, or maybe because its fear overwhelms it and it resorts to instinctual behavior no matter how much the rider knows about fighting tigers and lions. In that case, the rider's skills may be totally ignored and he loses control.

The elephant is like the old parts of our brain that control our strength and that react to fears, and the rider is like the more recent additions to our brain where planning, logic, and skills reside. What if the rider spends time training the elephant to react to threats in

Human nature, evolved instincts and culture—can we change?

a more controlled way? What if more training is given to both the rider and elephant so that their reactions are more synergistic and controlled? Perhaps the rider can guide the elephant to back carefully away in a defensive retreat. Perhaps the rider can carry a weapon. The point is that no matter what our automatic reactions may be, we can train and prepare ourselves to be more in control. This story can apply to many of our actions and has been utilized to help understand subconscious factors in drug seeking and addiction.[18]

With this story in mind, let us look at some other results of research. Studies of our mental processes suggest the presence of two systems in our brains that produce our actions, judgments, and thoughts. System one is always turned on, produces very automatic thoughts and answers, is intuitive, works quickly, takes little or no effort, and offers a fast guide to situations as they come up. An example is seeing the equation 1+1=? We automatically know that the answer is two. System one is great for rapid reactions and no doubt developed because it helps us survive, particularly in ancestral situations. System one and its responses are mainly what we have talked about so far in this chapter. System one doesn't care much about the accuracy or consequences of its actions.

But there is another process, system two, which is slower, lazier in a sense, and requires effort to engage. It is conscious, rule-based, and produces planned behavior and statistical awareness (i.e., what are my chances?). When you see 13X19=?, system two engages. It does calculations that require some effort. It has been suggested that system two has evolved more recently than system one, and different brain regions mediate the systems. Limbic and older brain regions carry system one and the frontal cortex carries system two. A nice thing about system two is that it can evaluate the action by system one. Both systems have some biases that produce errors, but engaging system two when judging or planning is a good idea because system two does a better job at these than system one. We can watch our own behaviors and see how system one works quickly, but it can be misleading. System two helps us be more rational and successful in our behaviors, particularly if there are complex issues. But remember that system two is somewhat lazy, and effort is required to use it. There has been a great deal of research on this.[19-21] Collegial ethics has benefited from this discovery. By learning to use system two, especially when the stakes are high, we maximize our chances of arriving at good solutions. It is not a good idea to accept only our immediate and instinctual reactions; system two needs a little time to kick in.

Are We Really Truly Rational In Our Responses?

Psychologists have studied human responses and decisions, and there have been some amazing findings. An outcome of behavioral studies has been the notion of a *confirmation bias*.[22,23] This bias means that we select information to support our *preconceptions*. For example, if we have come up with the idea, for whatever reason, that politicians are crooks, we tend to cite all the cases where that has been proven. But we also tend to ignore all of the evidence that does not support this idea. We try to make our positions look reasonable and supported by facts. However, this idea is not totally supported and reasonable because of the many politicians who are not crooks but rather honest public servants.

Also, our responses to situations can depend on how they are presented to us.[24] For example, suppose we are asked to vote for or against a new, expensive medical procedure directed at a disease that kills about five thousand people per year. The new procedure will save five hundred lives per year. Then we are told either that 1) it will save five hundred lives per year from death from disease, or that 2) it is an advance but will still not prevent 90 percent of the people with this illness from dying every year. People will respond to the first statement more positively than to the second because we prefer clear and positive statements of gains and not losses. Making a sound decision requires some time to look at the data from several perspectives.

Although our brains have done well enough to have produced our amazing civilization and an advanced society, our brains and their reasoning processes are not perfect, and we have known shortcomings and biases. Realizing and accepting this gives us pause. What is the best way to decide and react? Certainly, being aware of our shortcomings can help us be more open minded. We can react rapidly and automatically; this skill derives from ancient parts of our brains that are highly toned for survival. Another kind of reaction is a slower one (system 2 vs. system 1 as described above), one that allows us to utilize reason and rational thought. The latter may take some time to kick in, and it is clear that we shouldn't ignore this slower, more rational process.[24]

We can deceive ourselves, and this self-deception also has been studied. Self-deception is denying something even though there is evidence and logical arguments for it. It means that we convince ourselves of a lie so well that we do not reveal or show any knowledge of the lie or deception in our expression or demeanor.[25] It's amazing that we can do that. Examples of this might include a drug addict who says that he can quit drugs at any time even though he really hasn't been able to, or someone in such deep grief over a loss he or she just can't accept it, or a failure that we just can't accept and therefore attribute to another source. How do we do this and why? One notion is that this ability evolved in our psyches because it gives us an advantage. One can imagine many situations where deceiving another person could provide an advantage. One example could involve lying about the location of a source of food when food is very scarce. Another example may be lying about a newly discovered procedure, one that will bring wealth, until it is patented. But why is deceiving ourselves useful? The ability of *self*-deception helps us because, if we can convince *ourselves* that something is true, then we won't show *others* any signs of the deception we are perpetrating. If we believe it ourselves, we can more easily convince others. Human nature is an amazing thing.

Moral Reasoning After The Fact

Sometimes we are very rational, but in an unexpected way for unexpected reasons. Let it be said that first we respond and act instinctively and automatically to situations, and then we rationally justify our responses. Rational justification can come after, not before, an action. Some may not believe this, but many studies over many years have explored how we respond to our environment and act. More often than not, we respond automatically and quickly, and thinking about it follows later (maybe just seconds later). If we see or hear something that is automatically disgusting to us, we respond by avoiding or condemning it automatically and intuitively. When questioned about it, we bring up, conjure up really, moral reasons for our reactions. If those reasons are refuted, we search for new justifications. Consider a hospital worker who moves recently deceased patients to a morgue. One day, this worker who is short of groceries and cash, takes a piece of flesh home to cook and eat (This story is similar to one used in a research study). When people were asked about the morality of the situation, their innate disgust drove them to come up with reason after reason why it was morally wrong, even if the reason could be refuted. Their emotions came first and the reasons second. They didn't necessarily need reasons to justify their own personal disgust, but they searched for reasons to satisfy the questions of others (interviewers). The point here is that the reasons we give for some of our actions could ring of high morality and righteousness, but in fact may be due to other, very mundane factors. We need to be aware that we put intuitions and emotions first and conjured reasons second. This behavior has been recently summarized in a book on moral psychology.[26]

This tendency can play out in other ways. Suppose someone does something to someone else and is caught. For example, someone may invade another's privacy by looking into their possessions or past, out of simple curiosity. When the invasion is discovered, they are chastised and embarrassed, and - they react to this embarrassment by conjuring reasons to justify it. They exaggerate some of their findings and cast them in a bad light. Or perhaps they needlessly reveal past misdeeds of the colleague as a justification. They generate high moral reasons for the invasion which are far from the truth of simple curiosity. Sadly, when this happens, everyone ends up being hurt in some way. The person invaded is hurt because some might believe the exaggerations or at least doubt the person in some way. The person who invaded and justified the actions with conjured reasons is shunned because no one wants it done to them.

We behave this way because we are human. Being aware of this tendency to conjure moral reasons after mundane motives or actions can help us be more humble, self-aware, compassionate, and less judgmental.

"Attribution Errors"

Psychologists have studied how people respond to certain situations, and this has revealed how biased we can be in our responses. If we see something happen to another person, such as stubbing his or her toe, we tend to think that the reason this happened is because they are somehow personally responsible for it (e.g., they are clumsy or accident prone), rather than thinking that the situation rather than the person has blame (e.g., someone must have moved that couch). By solely attributing the cause of a mishap to the person's character or disposition, we make what is called the fundamental attribution error.[27] However, when we have a mishap—guess what!—we are more likely to attribute the situation's cause to someone or something else rather than to our own character. For example, someone may say, "I stubbed my toe because somebody moved that couch," or "I stubbed my toe because the light bulb was out and I couldn't see well." It is quite amazing that we all tend to respond that way. Whatever the reason for it, this kind of response sets us up to blame and judge others rather than to understand and offer help. Being aware of this in each of us can help us react to others and their problems in a more fair way.

Say It—Believe It

Suppose we believe that a certain something is right and correct, but others in your group don't agree, and are a bit pushy about it. In fact, they are so pushy that they try to get you to agree with them, and they want you to say you agree. They want you to contradict your real belief and say that it is *not* right and correct. Should you agree to their position even if you don't really agree with them? Can it hurt to give in to appease them? The answer to that is surprising. Studies show that if you *say* that you agree with them, even if you really don't, then your belief has moved in the direction of your colleagues' position. The simple act of *saying* that you believe something can weaken your belief, even if the pressure to do so is very mild.[28,29] What we say not only impacts others; it also impacts us. We need to be careful about what we put into words because language is the backbone of our involvement in groups and with colleagues, and we must honor and have courage about our real beliefs. Getting us to state something, perhaps something considered wrong about another, can be a tool of demonizers who want you to join them in being critical of another.

The Good Samaritan Experiment: Haste and Failure To Help

One of the most interesting studies about helping people has been called the Good Samaritan Experiment.[30] The study's organizers wanted to test our willingness to help others and the influence of certain factors on helping. These factors included the person's relative haste and hurry, and whether or not the person was occupied with other matters.

Religious studies students were used in the experiments, and they were told to travel from one building to the next. Some were told not to hurry, while others were told that speed was essential. One group was told that they would be giving lectures about life at their seminary, while others would be giving a lecture on the Good Samaritan. As you likely know, the Good Samaritan is a biblical story about helping someone who was in need.

Between the two buildings where the students had to travel was an "injured" man (not really injured, just part of the experiment). Observers noted how much assistance the students would offer during their movement from one building to the other. The results were quite amazing. Only one in ten of the students who were told to rush stopped to help, but two thirds of those without haste did stop. The students who were on their way to give a speech about the Good Samaritan were more likely to stop than the others, showing that what was on the students' minds influenced their behavior. But the major explanation for failing to help was how *hurried* they were. Even the students going to speak about the Good Samaritan were less likely to stop if they were in a hurry. Imagine the irony of a religious studies student going to teach about the Good Samaritan who steps right over a hurt person to get to the lecture. The degree of haste in our lives can influence how much we help others. On the positive side, ignoring the victim was not because they didn't care, but rather, it was about being pressured by their own haste. It also seems very likely that haste is not going to be the only factor influencing our actions. Therefore, many simple and practical demands can influence our actions, even when faced with someone who is hurt and needs help. Can we find more effective ways to deal with emergencies even when we are in a serious hurry?

Let Somebody Else Do It

On March 13, 1964, Kitty Genovese was stabbed to death near her home in Queens, New York City. As she was dying, she was raped and robbed. An early view of the murder posed by early newspaper accounts suggested that thirty-eight people were aware of it but did nothing to help. Subsequent investigations suggested that this was not exactly true, but it led to a series of psychological studies about what is called the "bystander effect" and "diffusion of responsibility." Contrary to expectations, the studies showed that a situation with a larger number of bystanders is less likely to produce assistance than if there are fewer bystanders. For various reasons, there is a diffusion of or lessening of responsibility when there are more people around witnessing an incident where someone needs help. They aren't apathetic or bad people; they are just less likely to act. Their reasons could be that they expect someone else to do it or that they were concerned how they might look to other bystanders if they did act.

We are often part of a *big* corporation or organization. If someone gets into trouble, the tendency is to stand by and do little or nothing. The closer you are to the situation, the more likely you are to act, but if you perceive yourself as one of many bystanders, then you are more likely to simply stand by and do little. Can we develop an approach where we can more effectively assess and analyze when and how we should act in these situations?

We Are Culturally Diverse

For example, what about cultural factors like relative wealth? Are the rich less empathetic and compassionate? You might suspect that the wealthy might be able to afford more empathy, but studies seem to show the opposite. Researchers at the University of California, Berkeley, and elsewhere have been testing to see whether people from different social backgrounds have different attitudes about empathy. Their results suggest that poorer people are warmer and more engaging, while the richer were more distant. Also, poorer subjects were better at understanding their partner's feelings.[31] The rich tend to be different in other ways as well. An unsettling, recent suggestion is that the rich are more likely to do something illegal while driving or cheat a little to win a prize.[32] These findings, coupled with data that the rich live longer and healthier, leave us concerned about the underprivileged.

Overall, it seems that social and financial success can influence our levels of caring. It's possible that we are not always aware of this fact. Perhaps if we are led to see the evidence and are counseled otherwise, we would react more empathetically. Also, not all of the wealthy act this way. On the contrary, to name just a few, Ted Turner, Bill Gates, and Warren Buffett all donate a substantial part of their wealth to philanthropic causes. Becoming aware of selfish, automatic behavior can lead to very collegial actions. This section was not included to poke at the rich, but only to show that a person's culture can influence his or her actions.

Bullying: Is It Only For Kids?

Bullying is aggressive behavior, directed at someone who is a target of abuse that can be emotional, verbal, or physical. It is usually a concern in schools where much has been said about it and about how to deal with it. Some states have been so concerned that they have created laws against it. The US Department of Health and Human Services has a website to identify and help those who are bullied.[33] But, bullying doesn't stop in schools. It graduates into adulthood, where it has been referred to as peer abuse, incivility, or verbal abuse.[34, 35] Is there any difference between teenagers saying nasty things and excluding a child who is a minority, and adults who push minorities aside or ignore them at a fancy restaurant in a good neighborhood? Some researchers feel that bullying is so common that people don't realize its harmful effects—including depression, anxiety, irritability, insecurity, high blood pressure, migraines, and more. Even psychiatrists, who understand abuse and its consequences, might behave in this way. These emotions are part of being human, although perhaps an unattractive part. It is believed that bullying breeds more bullying. In order to justify it and ignore it, it is sometimes mislabeled as a personality conflict. The question for us is what to do about it. How do we help ourselves or colleagues who are being bullied? How do we help the bullies? What part of human nature is behind it?

Perhaps it is ironically based on the drive to form safe groups and strong communities, and the person gets bullied because he is somehow labeled an outsider. We may treat outsiders badly because we don't want them to "contaminate" our community. Even though we may understand this underlying tendency in human nature, we cannot accept behavior that is unnecessarily damaging to others. Respect for others must be established by training and discipline if needed.[36, 37] There is a large literature on bullying.

Consider the following case of bullying, damage, and restitution. Dr. D is a professional who has done quite well in his career. He has won awards, is respected by many and has a strong clique of friends. However, in his later years, he begins to realize that he has made some significant errors. At times, he has been *anti-collegial* in that he has demonized and bullied colleagues that he didn't like or was told not to like. He would treat them poorly, was abusive, and tried to exclude them. By doing this, he harmed many of them and damaged heir reputations. He was not only a leader in these actions but also actually threatened those who wouldn't join him. It's as though he was locked into a continual hazing event, but it was far from harmless, as hazing can often be. He laughed off and blamed others for the problems that occurred. Even though a professional in the health care field, he never saw a problem with his behavior and was supported by his like-minded friends. However, over time, friends and colleagues became angry with him. When his wife left him and some colleagues disconnected from him, he began to understand the pattern he has been in for many years. Going as far back as his college days he showed a certain meanness, selfishness and callousness. He wonders if he has some sociopathic tendencies. But, even though

Dr. D is beginning to realize what he has done, he is afraid to discuss it and admit to it. At times, he is obsessed with his error. Also, he is afraid of retribution from those he hurt so he doesn't want to face it. What can Dr. D do to restore a positive balance in his "ethical bank account?"

While Dr. D cannot take back the damage he has done over the years, it seems he can do at least two things. One is to make restitution as best he can, and two, he can examine his failures and adopt better behaviors and attitudes in the future. Restitution may be significant because he has done serious harm to some, and Dr. D may be afraid to face that. But restitution can be more than money. It can be an apology and service, for example. Because of the potential anger of those he has hurt, he may have to be *creative* about this and how to restore a positive balance to his ethical bank account.

What does he need to change and focus on? What mistakes did he make? Certainly avoiding personal responsibility for hurtful actions is one. Showing a lack of compassion and empathy is another. In collegial ethics, does simply *disliking* someone ever justify destructive behavior? If he was *told* to act this way by others, does this show a lack of personal responsibility and *courage*? What kind of program can he adopt to develop more responsibility, courage, compassion and empathy? Perhaps he can get counseling, seek mentoring, read about people who have the qualities he desires, and persist in trying to develop collegial habits.

Can We Change?

Can we change and become more courageous, thoughtful, compassionate, and collegial? The answer is an emphatic *yes*. Although there are limits to change, we certainly can alter much of our behaviors by choice and training.

There are training programs for just about everything. There are colleges, technical schools, professional schools, engineering schools, and classes for everything from management to languages. The point is that training programs of all kinds exist, and they exist because they are successful. This in itself is abundant evidence that we can and do grow and change.

Soldiers and law enforcement officers are trained to react almost automatically to fear, attacks, an injured colleague, or other situations. Without the training, you might be unable to act or you might misjudge the situation and either over- or under react. Soldiers and law enforcement officers are not only prepared to deal with the consequences, they are also prepared to react to consequences in a planned and constructive way. Their training comes from a combination of classroom and field work where they act out and practice responses and actions. They study relevant or case work to learn from other's mistakes and successes. In the field, colleagues and superiors review their actions and adjust them if need be. Their training and practice bring about striking changes. Because they deal with extreme and life threatening situations, their training must be rigorous and intense. Fortunately, you probably don't need to invest as much as a law enforcement officer to be a good colleague, but you might follow the same *kind* of training plan, even if it is less extensive and consuming.

Sometimes change occurs over generations. In the 1980s, a philosophy about child rearing developed that emphasized boosting children's self-esteem independent of their actions. A study reported that in 2009, 52 percent of college freshmen said they had a level of self-confidence higher than the average in the population. This compared with 30 percent in 1966. So, maybe the new philosophy is working. Like any change, there is both positive and negative effects. Some feel that this change has made kids today spoiled and feeling entitled. We'll have to see if the increased confidence and esteem are worth it or not. In any case, this change has affected families and schools nationwide.

Just a hundred years ago, most people in this country lived on farms. Today, most people live in cities. This is a huge change in a relatively short time. There are fewer person-to-person interactions on farms and a need for physical work. One hundred years ago, there was less media and less access to goods. In cities, people confront great numbers of people every day. Their work is less likely to be physical, and they rely on computer skills to a great degree. Availability of cell phones and the Internet has speeded communication as if there were no distance between colleagues. People have an almost infinite choice of goods around them or through the Internet. These changes are as radical as we could imagine—a hundred years ago, we probably couldn't imagine them. Yet they have happened, and we are coping with them and even enjoying them. Our learning and adaptations have worked and have been successful. These changes can be very challenging for those who are older, but young people seem very adapted to cell phones and computers, for example. Who knows what kind of changes are in store for us in the future?

Not only can we change, but we also have figured out some of the factors that can facilitate change. These factors include rewards and punishments. Rewards can produce change very effectively if they are great enough and if they are given soon enough after the action. If they are not very big, and if they are given long after the action, then the effect of the reward will be weakened, and there may be no change. For example, consider that we are given the task of learning a new dance step, one that we haven't seen before. We are also rewarded with two hundred dollars immediately after we try the new step. We are given twice as much, if the judges believe we do it well. Of course, we'll do the step; the worst we can do is get two hundred dollars. Now, what happens if the reward is ten cents? Perhaps we won't want to show how clumsy we are, and we'll pass. What if the reward is ten cents, and we get the ten cents next year, not immediately? Most people wouldn't even stop to consider it. Punishments can work the same way. They can inhibit an undesirable behavior if they are great enough and implemented soon enough so that they are connected to the action. We can use this knowledge by giving ourselves effective rewards when we do what we want, and punishments when we don't. The rewards could be some extra time having fun or some extra spending money. Interestingly, the punishments could be things that are ultimately *good* for us, such as more exercise or dieting. This approach utilizes our human nature to produce a desirable change. In collegial ethics, the changes might be learning to listen better rather than just talking about yourself, making a compassionate statement rather than a judgmental one, or standing up for your own opinions in a group. The human brain, the organ of our behaviors, is a learning machine, and we can use that.

Some of us may not need to change much. Compassion, altruism, courage, and other collegial personality traits are often abundant in our colleagues. Where do they come from? Are they learned or inherited or both? They are presumably learned, but they seem to be inherited to some extent as well. Some of the evidence for this comes from studying our closest nonhuman relatives, the chimpanzees. These animals often console each other, particularly when they are very distressed. Female chimps are reported to put their arms around a distressed fellow until it stops screaming. It is not just our human culture that produces altruism; its roots may be deeper than that and in our biology.[38, 39] Then why the concern, and why address the need for training? Our tendencies for altruism and consoling are highly variable among individuals. Some express it often, while others don't. So, the training may not necessarily be in learning altruism itself, but rather in learning how to express and amplify what is already inside us, however deep.

The Bottom Line

Our evolved instincts have no doubt contributed to our survival and our successes as humans. This is not being denied, but only qualified in the sense that our automatic, instinctual responses are not *always* helpful. When we look at this chapter and the previous one, there is little wonder that we sometimes do not help colleagues. We understand ourselves and human nature so poorly that we can be confused and afraid. We tend to be obedient to authority even if someone is being hurt. Being in a hurry motivates us to abandon the needy. The bottom line is that our very nature and culture can keep us on the sidelines when perhaps we should be acting. It's not that we are good or bad; we are just human. Many of us are not experienced or trained to react in a collegial way. How do we overcome this and be freer to help if we choose to? How do we increase our available options rather than be bound in natural tendencies because of evolution and culture? First, an awareness of the problem is key, and this will be covered in more detail later. Through research and study, we continue to learn about our natural tendencies, our fast (system one) and slow (system two) thinking, and this is good. There are many examples of how our fears and tendencies have been overcome and how we can change through training. In some ways, change is well understood. But we probably aren't as far along as we would like.

It is clear that through no fault of our own, we have a complex human nature. Part of it is collegial and part of it isn't. But, it is also clear that we *can* modify our actions and behaviors and become more collegial.

Notes for Chapter 3

1. "Deepak Chopra." Goodreads, accessed on July 12, 2012, from http://www.goodreads.com/quotes/tag/evolution.

2. accessed on October 27, 2012, http://thepersonaldevelopmentcompany.typepad.com/my-blog/2012/10/to-change-the-world-start-with-yourself.html

3. Dawkins, R. *The Greatest Show on Earth*, (New York: Free Press, 2009).

4. Rogers, A. R. *The Evidence for Evolution*, (Chicago: University of Chicago Press, 2011).

5. Symons, D. *The Evolution of Human Sexuality*. Oxford: Oxford University Press.1979.

6. Cosmides, L. and J. Tooby. D. M. Buss (Ed)"Evolutionary Psychology: Conceptual Foundations." *Evolutionary Psychology Handbook*. (New York: Wiley, 2005).

7. Darwin, C. *The Expression of the Emotions in Man and Animals*. (Chicago: University of Chicago Press, 1965).

8. Kurzban, R. and M. R. Leary. "Evolutionary Origins of Stigmatization: The Function of Social Exclusion," *Psychological Bulletin* 127 (2001): 187–208.

9. Allen, N. B. and P. B. T. Badcock. "The Social Risk Hypothesis of Depressed Mood: Evolutionary, Psychosocial and Neurological Perspectives," *Psychological Bulletin* 129 (2003): 887–913.

10. Allen, N. B. and P. B. T. Badcock. "Darwinian Models of Depression: A Review of Evolutionary Accounts of Mood and Mood Disorders," *Progress in Neuro-Psychopharmacology and Biological Psychiatry*. 30 (2006): 815–826.

11. Gilbert, P. "The Evolved Basis and Adaptive Functions of Cognitive Distortions," *British Journal of Medical Psychology* 71 (1998): 447–463.

12. Kenrick, D. T., S. L. Neuberg, and M. Schaller. "Human Threat Management Systems: Self-Protection and Disease Avoidance," *Neuroscience & Biobehavioral Reviews* March 35(4) (2011): 1042–51.

13. "The Full-Blown American Optimist," *New Scientist* (April 21, 2012): 34.

14. Milgram S. "Behavioral Study of Obedience," *J Abn and Soc Psych* (1963) 67: 371-378.

15. Milgram S. *Obedience to authority: An experimental view.* (New York: Perennial, 1983)

16. Blass T. (Ed) *Obedience to authority: current perspectives on the Milgram Paradigm* (Mahwah, NJ: Lawrence Erlbaum Associates, 2000).

17. Haidt, Jonathan. *The Happiness Hypothesis: Finding Modern Truth in Ancient Wisdom.* New York, NY. (Basic Books, 2006).

18. Kuhar, MJ. *The Addicted Brain.* (Upper Saddle River: FT Press, 2011).

19. accessed on 8/25/2012, Of Two Minds When Making a Decision. http://www.scientificamerican.com/article.cfm?id=of-two-minds-when-making.

20. Kahneman, D. *Thinking, Fast and Slow.* (New York: Farrar, Straus and Giroux, 2011).

21. accessed on 8/25/2012, Two System Thinking. http://tim-reidpartnership.com/Site/An_introduction_to_2_system_thinking.html.

22. Lodge, M., A. A. Strickland, and C. S. Taber. "Motivated Reasoning and Public Opinion," *Journal of Health Politics, Policy and Law* 36(6) (December 2011): 935–944.

23. Mercier, H. and D. Sperber. "Why Do Humans Reason? Arguments for an Argumentative Theory," *Behavioral and Brain Sciences* 34(2) (April 2011): 57–74, 74–111.

24. Kahneman, D. and A. Tversky. "The Framing of Decisions and the Psychology of Choice," *Science* 30; 211(4481) (January 1981): 453–458.

25. Culotta, E. "Roots of Racism," *Science* 336 (2012): 825–827.

26. Haidt, J. *"The Righteous Mind: Why Good People are Divided by Politics and Religion."* (New York: Vintage Books, 2012).

27. Harris, V. A. and E. E. Jones. "The Attribution of Attitudes," *Journal of Experimental Social Psychology* 3(1) (1967): 1–24.

28. Carlsmith, J. M. and L. Festinger. "Cognitive Consequences of Forced Compliance," *Journal of Abnormal and Social Psychology* 58 (1959): 203–210.

29. Gawronski, B. and F. Strack. "On the Propositional Nature of Cognitive Consistency: Dissonance Changes Explicit, but not Implicit Attitudes," *Journal of Experimental Social Psychology* 40 (2004): 535–542.

30. Baston, C. D. and J. M. Darley. "From Jerusalem to Jericho: A Study of Situational and Dispositional Variables in Helping Behavior," *Journal of Personality and Social Psycholgy* 27 (1973): 100–108.

31. Côté, S., D. Keltner, and M. W. Kraus. "Social Class, Contextualism, and Empathic Accuracy," *Psychological Science* 21(11) (November 2010, ePub October 25, 2010):1716–1723.

32. Côté, S., D. Keltner, R. Mendoza-Denton, P. K. Piff, and D. M. Stancato. "Higher Social Class Predicts Increased Unethical Behavior," *Proceedings of the National Academy of Sciences* 109(11) (March 13, 2012, ePub February 27, 2012): 4086–4091.

33. accessed on June 7, 2012, *http://www.stopbullying.gov/*.

34. Jagatic, K. and L. Keashly. "By Any Other Name: American Perspectives on Workplace Bullying," *Workplace Emotional Abuse Bullying and Emotional Abuse in the Workplace: International Perspectives in Research and Practice.* (London: Taylor Francis, 2003): 31–61.

35. accessed on Sept 10, 2012 Office bullies. *http://www.apa.org/monitor/julaug06/index.aspx*.

36. Gault, D. "Creating Respectful, Violence-Free, Productive Workplaces: A Community-Level Response to Workplace Violence," *Journal of Emotional Abuse* 4 (2005): 119–138.

37. Keashly, L. and J. H. Neuman. "Reducing Aggression and Bullying: An Intervention Project in the US Department of Veterans Affairs," *Workplace Bullying: International Perspectives on Moving from Research to Practice.* Symposium conducted at the meeting of the Academy of Management, Honolulu, HI, August 2005.

38. Choi, CQ. "Simian Solicitude: Like Humans, Chimpanzees Console Victims of Aggression," *Scientific American*, (June 14, 2010). http://www.scientificamerican.com/article.cfm?id=humans-chimpanzees-console-victims-of-aggression

39. Romero T, Castellanos MA, de Waal FB. "Consolation as Possible Expression of Sympathetic Concern among Chimpanzees," *Proceedings of the National Academy of Sciences* 107(27) (Jul 6, 2010, ePub June 14, 2010): 12110–12115.

Part II

Becoming Collegial

4

Getting Involved and Being Supportive.

It is one of the most beautiful compensations of life, that no man can sincerely try to help another without helping himself.
 —Ralph Waldo Emerson[1]

Courage is resistance to fear, mastery of fear—not absence of fear." —Mark Twain[2]

It is not the mountain we conquer but ourselves.
 —Edmund Hillary[3]

What does support mean? As was described earlier, the dictionary definition is: "promoting, or upholding, or defending, or helping." In collegial ethics, we support others when we can, and support can take many forms. We can even support people who have done destructive things and broken the law by pushing for appropriate, rehabilitative, and corrective action. What footing do we stand on when we offer support? Do we stand on legalities, cultural norms, public opinion, or something else? Given all the choices, it seems that our position will depend on the situation.

Empathy, compassion and mercy are inherent in supporting others. They can have a higher value than strict, legal justice. Some have argued that compassion has a proper place in the law and even enhances the law.[4] For example, a Texas judge refused to consider eviction cases in the weeks before Christmas and instead heard them in January; he wanted to avoid heartbreak in the children of these families.[5]

A cornerstone of collegial ethics is that our actions have an *impact* on others. If we don't act, there may be a significant impact anyway. In a sense, not acting is still a form of acting. We often don't realize the impact we have on others. We don't understand why others can become upset over something we say or do. Some may say that we can't be responsible for how others react to us. But in collegial ethics, it is fundamental that we need to be concerned about our impact on others in order to be a good colleague. Our impact may depend on subtle interactions. Not only do the contents of our words count, but it also matters how we say them.

Obviously, being supportive will take some time and attention. We have to focus on another person for a little while. If collegial ethics had a motto, then it would be, "Give a little time." Spending time on developing supportive skills and appropriate actions is essential for being a good colleague. Spending time to listen to others is important. Spending time to assess a situation and deciding on how to get involved is fundamental to ethics.

Judging The Situation

This is number one. When confronted with a colleague or situation that may need attention, judgment is where we begin and it must compete with any emotion that we feel. What will be the outcome if I get involved, and what will happen if I don't; this process of forecasting will be central in the decision. During the forecast, don't forget to examine the positive outcomes; fear can be so powerful that it may tend to push your forecasting into the realm of how can I get hurt rather than how can I help.

Here is the kind of thinking that would be beneficial. What is the best thing that will happen if I get involved? What is an appropriate way to support this colleague in this situation?" Should I get involved just because I'm a decent human being and because the colleague needs help? Will I be in some kind of jeopardy if I get involved? What do I lose if I don't get involved, and is it worth the consequences? Are there legal and ethical issues that must be considered? Is the colleague using your collegial efforts for their own gain which may be inappropriate? Psychopathic behavior and how it can affect us is discussed in Chapter 7. There are limits to collegiality. Sound judgment requires addressing all of these questions and more. Perhaps discussions with colleagues can help this process.

Judging right from wrong is not always easy. Sometimes what is right for one person may not be right for another person. While this makes things more complicated, it would be foolish not to admit that values in life can sometimes be ambiguous and depend on situations and cultures. Collegial ethics admits to ambiguities in right and wrong in some cases—and that may influence how we support others—but it still requests that we support others as best we can. Consider someone who has an unusual and incurable fatal disease. The person has a right to prolong his useful life as much as possible, as he has dependents and contributes much to others. But suppose the life-extending treatments are experimental, extraordinarily expensive, not certain to produce the results he wants, and may be toxic. The medical profession and policy makers also have a right to reasonably limit medical care expenses because we all pay for them, and attempting to prolong life in this case would be extraordinarily expensive, difficult, and uncertain. So both sides are "right" from their own perspectives, but the consequences for each are very different. Because of the situation's limitations that can't be overcome, simply listening to another person with compassion and empathy may be the best thing you can do.

It is interesting that legal guilt or innocence is not the same as ethical guilt or innocence. According to the law, we are innocent until guilt is proven. If guilt cannot be proven, then we are officially not guilty. But if we really committed a wrong, we are, in fact, ethically guilty, and an ethical debt has been incurred. Right and wrong in ethics is based on what actually happened rather than on what can be proven in a court of law.

After judging the situation and deciding to get involved, how can we help most effectively? Again, this will depend on our position and whether we have the skills needed which are discussed in later chapters.

What Will It Cost Me?

In simple, everyday interactions with colleagues, it might cost very little to be supportive. It can be something as small as an approving glance or a simple gesture, or it could involve an extended conversation over a meal. If a colleague loses a parent, you can take the person to lunch and let him or her talk. If a colleague is struggling with something you can readily solve, you can help out. If you hear negative gossip about someone, you can rightfully question it if you know the real facts. If someone is stuck in a hospital recuperating, sending them a cheerful card; visiting can really brighten the person's day. However, there are situations where it could be costly to be supportive. The cost could be financial, time taken, risk of damage, or emotional stress and energy. Knowing how much to commit to a colleague or situation can take some thought. Can the consequences of getting involved cost you too much? Maybe so. This is an important question because we all have limitations in our time, energy, and resources, and we must consider each situation separately.

How Close Am I To The Situation?

When something happens, how close you are to the situation will be an important factor. We can have several degrees of proximity to a situation. One degree would be where you have no relationship to the colleagues involved. You may not know them or their situation very well and rarely, if ever, see them. In this case, offering support would require going out of your way to even say hello. We all have limitations in time and energies. Nevertheless, you may need to be involved if the stakes are high for you. Another degree of proximity would be where you have some level of personal involvement. Maybe the colleague is in your division or is a neighbor. Now you can be supportive more easily, and the issues could affect you more directly than if you were very distant.

The most proximal degree is when you are directly involved. There are many ways that this could happen. One is a direct rivalry. Both you and a colleague are pursuing the same thing, such as a new job, recognition, or even a love interest. You may need to "fight" back or try to win, but ethics say you have to do it fairly. A challenge for collegial ethics is to be collegial but yet allow for appropriate competition and debate. Another situation is where you are hurting and very shook up, maybe because of an accusation or by a serious failure. You are now likely to experience firsthand the need for collegiality and help.

It is interesting that we don't necessarily have to wait for a "situation" to happen to be supportive. In the year 2000, a movie entitled *Pay it Forward* with Kevin Spacey and Haley Joel Osment used the phrase "pay it forward" as a way to make the world a better place. Paying it forward suggests that when we are the recipient of a good deed, then we should do a good deed for others (even strangers) without being asked. What would the reaction be in the workplace if you and your colleagues did this? Remember the saying, "Practice random acts of kindness and senseless acts of beauty"?

Courage—The Missing Ingredient

We can have wide-ranging experiences, sound judgment, and great moral foundations, but unless we know how *to act* on an issue, *all that is wasted*. Sometimes it is clear that we should act but we don't, and chapters 2 and 3 covered some of the reasons why we might not. This is where a very important ingredient, *courage,* comes into play. It is often the critical and missing factor in many ethical situations, and one of the most important skills in collegiality. Can we develop it? Yes, we can. Reasonable ways to develop courage are given in the next chapter.

The acronym CODE has been used to remind us of the elements of courage. C is for courage itself and what it requires. O is for our obligation to do the right thing. Many organizations include courage and obligations to others in their codes of ethics.[6,7] D is for danger management or how I deal with my fear. E is for the expression of action, which reflects our courage and obligations.

Einstein said: "The world is a dangerous place, not because of those who do evil, but because of those who look on and do nothing."[8] Courage is so important that we need to understand it better. Is it fearless action? Hardly. Aristotle spoke of courage, and he said that it was a balance between the extremes of cowardice and rashness. He wrote, "He is courageous who endures and fears the right things, for the right motive, in the right manner, and at the right time and who displays confidence in a similar way." Courage is the ability to overcome (or accept) fear and act according to one's values. It can require risk, and that can be a problem for those who only play it safe. Part of developing courage means accepting the circumstances and acting in spite of risk to us. In our culture, courage doesn't seem to be stressed. In fact, the opposite seems to prevail. "Mind your own business, and go along and get along" is what we often hear. Our culture can and certainly should modify its views on this point.

Sometimes courage clearly exists but goes by another name. Members of our armed forces or civil servants like firemen believe in the idea of "no man left behind." In other words, if a colleague is injured, you do anything you can to get him to safety. In doing this, we see acts of amazing courage, but when the heroes are questioned, they say, "I was just doing my job." Or they might say, "I needed to be there for my buddies." In these cases, it seems that the *culture* of these men and women promote acts of courageous heroism, even when it could lead to serious injury for themselves. Of course, in our day-to-day lives, we don't face similar kinds of dangers; but the point is that if we can generate a culture of collegiality, then fear is less likely to prevent courageous actions. Sometimes this culture exists, but much more could be done to promote it in our society. Collegial ethics would be a useful guide for building, utilizing, and expanding a culture of courage.

Fortunately, courage is being recognized, at least a little. There are even prizes for courageous actions outside of law enforcement and the military. A web search brings up the Maddox prize and civil courage prizes. Perhaps we need more mechanisms for rewarding courage in everyday life.

Dale Carnegie's Heritage

Dale Carnegie was an important pioneer in helping people interact. In 1936, he wrote a book entitled *How to Win Friends and Influence People*. The book was hugely successful and made life easier and more pleasant for those who read and used it. Some very powerful and successful people have been impacted by Carnegie. It is said that Warren Buffett, the financier, studied and practiced Dale Carnegie's ideas. The book has become less popular in our era and has many competitors, but it still sells.

Carnegie's ideas overlap with collegial ethics. For example, he suggests genuinely appreciating others, trying to see things from their points of view, praising others' improvements, being encouraging, and making it seem that problems are easy to correct. If you talk about a person, then attribute a fine reputation to that person so that he will have one to live up to.[9] This approach has proven to be very powerful.

But collegial ethics may be slightly different in a key way. *How to Win Friends and Influence People* is primarily another way of showing you how to increase your personal power. For example, the benefits include increasing your popularity, winning people over to your way of thinking, making you a better salesman, etc. Collegial ethics primarily has the colleague's best interest in mind. Collegial ethics is primarily for the other person's sake, although we all have much to gain from a more collegial world. Colleagues may resent your actions if they think you are out to advance your own agenda.

Tolerance

Tolerance is basic to collegiality. We're familiar with religious, political, and racial tolerance. It's been said that if you lack tolerance, then you are just another kind of bigot. "Cherish diversity" has been the rallying cry against intolerance. Sometimes people comment in a self-righteous way about how others live. "I couldn't live that way," they say. But this response is judgmental and narrow minded in most cases. This statement implies that the speaker has the answer or knows how to live. Some people are so sure they are the ones who know how to live, that they commit mass suicide or even become suicide bombers. These examples are more extreme, but clearly cultivating tolerance would reduce this extreme behavior. On what do we base tolerance? After all, everyone is not equal in how they perform. Although it is true that the ability to perform is not the same for everyone, their *intrinsic worth* is the same. It is agreed that some people are better at math and some are better as athletes. Some are better businessmen than others as well. But if we can act in such a way that everyone has the same intrinsic worth as every other human being, then tolerance will have a strong basis.

Does tolerance have its limits? Of course it does. We can't be unquestionably tolerant of those who are destructive to us or others.

Institutional Problems

Sometimes we may face an institutional or hierarchical problem. For example, one of your colleagues is being investigated by your company and has been put on leave until the situation is resolved. Further, the company lawyers say that no one should have any contact with the person until things are resolved. This may be for very good reasons and benefit everyone. In cases like this, the devil is in the details. As usual, you will need to analyze and judge the situation before considering any action. If you decide to be active in a situation like this, you may get into a conflict with your boss, and no one wants to get on the boss's bad side. But bosses must be fair and reasonable. Good bosses will listen to employees. After all, they usually want to keep their employees.

In hierarchies, there is not simple equality, so collegiality will be different. It doesn't have to be absent but it will be different. It may be manifested by respect and compassion on the part of both the boss and the employees. Being the boss is not always easy. He can be perfect for 364 days, but if he makes a mistake on day 365, the only thing people remember is that day and the mistake. It isn't fair, but it is human nature. Negative events tend to have more emotional impact than positive ones. Bosses need for us to cut them some slack and be tolerant of their particular managerial styles and sometime errors. Being an active, supportive colleague when there are hierarchical issues can be complicated. Remember the section on obedience in chapter 3. Bosses have power that shouldn't be abused, and the workers need to be vigilant. More will be said about this in chapter 7.

What If *You* Are The One That Needs Help?

What do you do if you are the one in need of help? Remember the nightmare scenario in chapter 1? What if that applied to you? You could apply all of the same ideas and efforts to your own problem as if it were someone else's problem. Can you be collegial toward yourself? You probably can. Each situation may be different and call for a different response. Remember that because of your human nature, you are just as susceptible as others to deceiving and misleading yourself. Find someone to talk to who can be your sounding board. Judge what solutions are best. Be realistic and respond in proportion to the threat. Show the necessary courage in your responses and ask for help if needed. The skills you learn to help others later in this book can be just as useful to you in an adverse situation.

The Bottom Line

Being a good colleague requires spending a little time on collegial issues. In addition to devoting time, judgment and courage are also foundations of collegial ethics. Sound judgment will include a forecast or listing of the possible outcomes, and a consideration of which ones are most desirable and feasible. What will offering support cost me? Courage is often the missing ingredient in collegiality, and courage can be developed. Sometimes it is essential for our ability to act. Practicing tolerance is an important factor in collegial ethics. Legal and hierarchical issues may complicate but not eliminate collegial considerations.

Notes for Chapter 4

1. "Ralph Waldo Emerson" accessed on July 12, 2012, http://www.values.com/inspirational-quotes/value/25-Helping-Others/.

2. "Mark Twain," accessed on July 12, 2012, http://thinkexist.com/quotations/courage/3.html.

3. "Edmund Hillary," accessed on July 12, 2012, http://www.quotegarden.com/hang-in.html.

4. Avgoustinos C. "The Compassionate Judge. Public Space," *The Journal of Law and Social Justice* volume 1 (2007): 1–41.

5. accessed on June15, 2012, http://www.chron.com/news/falkenberg/article/The-name-of-judge-s-crime-is-compassion-1752813.php.

6. Lachman, V.D. "Moral Courage: A Virtue in Need of Development?" *MedSurg Nursing Journal* 16(2) (2007): 131–133.

7. Lachman, V.D. "Strategies Necessary for Moral Courage," *The Online Journal of Issues in Nursing*. 15(3) (2010): manuscript 3.

8. St. Peter, Anthony. *The Greatest Quotes of All Time*. (Bloomington: Xlibris Corp., 2010).

9. "Dale Carnegie," accessed on Feb 20, 2012), (http://en.wikipedia.org/wiki/How_to_Win_Friends_and_Influence_People

5

Collegial Skills: Language, Guidelines, and Behavior

Training is everything. The peach was once a bitter almond; cauliflower is nothing but cabbage with a college education.
—Mark Twain[1]

To me it seems that to give happiness is a far nobler goal that to attain it: and that what we exist for is much more a matter of relations to others than a matter of individual progress: much more a matter of helping others to heaven than of getting there ourselves. —Lewis Carroll[2]

Talking about collegial ethics and being supportive is useful, but how do we *implement* collegial ethics? How do we learn these skills? There is probably not a single answer or method, but we can look at other ethics programs and see what approaches they use. What skills do they focus on, and how do they teach the skills?

After examining various approaches, a reasonable way to teach collegial ethics is to (1) identify skills and principles for being collegial, (2) illustrate and clarify these skills and principles by collecting, studying and discussing examples (cases), (3) role-play, practice, critique, and replay, 4) review and discuss ongoing collegial problems,

(5) develop courses that present principles, cases, and exercises for efficient learning, and (6) develop mentors. This general approach has been effective for teaching professional ethics in graduate schools,[3] and this book utilizes this approach.

Many of these skills do not come naturally and have to be learned and practiced. Practice by yourself or, preferably, with others. If certain behaviors are very foreign to you, you can learn by role-playing in front of colleagues or in front of a camera. Either way you can practice and get more comfortable using these skills. Or you can look for a mentor. One-on-one training with someone you like and respect can be a good way to go. While not a complete list, the following sections describe some of the skills and principles that will help us be collegial.

Practice Being Positive and Uplifting To Others

This is often very simple and even fun. Consider a fictional Dr. Luckie who is nominated by a colleague for a teaching award; Dr. Luckie wins it and is surprised because he had never won any recognition before, even though he always has been thought of as an excellent teacher. Dr. Luckie wants to share the goodwill he feels, and he does this in various ways. When a lecturer he knows is being criticized, Dr. Luckie praises him for the positive parts of his presentation. He, good naturedly and with a smile, volunteers to help another professor run a demonstration for students. He brings small treats to the administrative staff in his department and tells them what a good job they've done. He shows appreciation publically. Small actions such as these can have an impact on others, and we sometimes underestimate what our *impact* can be.[4, 5]

Have you ever experienced people who are fun to work with? We all have. Watch how they do it. When they are working, they have a smile and a positive attitude. They find benign humor even in setbacks, and they are generous to others. It's important to remember

Collegial skills: language, guidelines, and behavior   73

that even small things can be uplifting and have an impact on others. You could say that positive *impact* is what collegial ethics is all about and you wouldn't be wrong too often. We can forget how powerful we are in relation to others. Little things can brighten moods. Little things such as assistance, encouragement, and sharing insights can sometimes help another person succeed.

Sometimes it's important to examine depressing and difficult issues with your colleagues. But maybe you could avoid those unrelated things that are a turnoff. Don't automatically dwell on negatives, rehash your own depressing problems, or unnecessarily raise embarrassing or depressing issues. Lightening up can be helpful to your colleagues.

Develop A Supportive and/or Neutral Language

Language is one of our most powerful tools and certainly accounts for much of the evolutionary success of our species, *Homo sapiens*. Language can do many things; it has the power to heal and calm, or it can inflame and anger. *It has impact.* Many groups recognize the power of language and have sought to mold it (for example, the Institute for Nonviolent Communication). We have seen many effects of language, haven't we? It isn't surprising that language is one of the most important tools for collegial support.

Although language has great power, we need to be aware of its limitations and inadequacies. This may be surprising to some, but our words do have limitations. Some poets feel that words are inadequate to fully express feelings. For example, can a word truly express the horror of the holocaust? Our need to convey a particular emotion is evident by the way we sometimes add a special inflection or stress to certain words to emphasize their meaning. Someone might say, "It was sooooo horrible," meaning that it was not just horrible but extraordinarily horrible. Some languages have multiple words for one concept whereas others don't. French has at least two words for language, "langue" and "langage," with slightly different meanings, whereas English has only the one. Eskimos have a long list of single words for different kinds of snow that can only be described in English with more than one word. For example, we use two words to describe "powder snow" while the Eskimos use a single word, "tlapa." Snow that has melted and refrozen is "kripya."[6] In his book on nonviolent communication, Marshall Rosenberg[7] includes lists of words to help us express the various nuances of our feelings. The point is that verbal communication can have its shortcomings, and finding the most accurate way to express something may be more of a challenge than we think. It may take some time and practice to learn new skills for expressing ourselves. Maybe we all can't do it perfectly, but we can all improve.

One of the things needed is the development of a supportive or at least neutral style of talking to or about colleagues. The following case exemplifies this.

A colleague has come under investigation regarding expenditures of his grant funds. He has a flawless track record, and the investigation has surprised everyone. A group of faculty members are discussing this in the dining hall (the colleague under investigation is not there).

"Hey Fred, you know this guy best, what did he do?"

Fred replies, "I have no idea."

Someone else says, "He must have done something to get investigated."

"Yeah, didn't he get a new car recently?" Everyone laughs at the intended humor.

"He hasn't shown his face lately."

"Yeah, sounds like guilty behavior to me."

"I'm going to stay away from him or else I might get investigated." There are a few serious nods and introspective faces around the table.

Now consider this alternative conversation.

"Hey Fred, you know this guy the best, what is happening?"

"I'm not sure. The alleged charges are being investigated, so I don't know. Maybe he did something bad. But it could be a misunderstanding or maybe something minor. I've seen that before."

"Where's he been? We haven't seen him."

"I think he feels bad, and maybe he's ashamed because of the investigation. But I think I'll give him a call and invite him to join us one of these days. Not so we can grill him, but so he can explain if he wants to. If he has made a mistake, then I'd like to learn from it."

It's obvious which conversation is more supportive. Does competition in the workplace—a positive force in many ways—set us up to be harsh to others? Probably so. Does human nature want us to deflate others in a self-aggrandizing way and even to enjoy their misfortune (schadenfreude)? Perhaps yes. But again, our learned and natural tendencies may not always be appropriate for every situation.[8] Collegial ethics could help us keep impulses driven by competition more under control.

We have all heard trash talk. It's a form of degrading or belittling other people, sometimes in good humor. But because of the impact our words can have, it's not always a good idea. It's often practiced by sports players who are competitors, and it is not supportive. So how do we respond to trash talk? If it is clearly a joke and not damaging, then maybe it is no big deal. However, if impressionable younger colleagues hear it, it may be adopted by them as a style of talking—which is not a great idea. If the trash talk we hear is damaging, then we should make our response to it very clear. Don't laugh and support it. Somehow show your displeasure. Now, what if your boss does it? What if he belittles an employee? The problems with bosses and hierarchies in collegial ethics are discussed in more detail elsewhere in this book. But when a boss does that, it adds a new dimension, even if he means it as a joke. Because of his position, words take on a greater significance. While there may be little we can do to stop it, we can at least not respond to it or encourage it. Again, we sometimes forget that we have an impact on those around us. And don't forget: The *way* we say things—our posture or expressions—very much influence what people think we mean. Our behavior is simply another language.

Another issue related to how we talk about others is *demonization*. Sometimes people who do not deserve it are demonized. Demonizing someone typically refers to making broad, negative, and demeaning comments about the person. "He's got a terrible reputation." "She's hated." "He doesn't belong here." "She's always in trouble." Demonizing is rarely intended or taken as a joke. It is often intended to damage someone so that a bad impression is given and will persist. Because it is general, lacks specific information, and is condemning, demonizing is a questionable practice. What can we do about this? When we hear someone being demonized, we can ask for facts that explain or support the comment. Being concrete and specific can force the discussion into a less global and more realistic arena. We could try to turn the conversation in a constructive direction by asking how the person could fix the problem and redeem him or herself. Or ask the demonizers what they would do if they were in that situation.

There are probably many underlying reasons for demonization. It may be that something has made someone angry, or there may be a clash of values. Another could be that the demonizers are armoring themselves, carrying out a self-deception, to avoid feeling guilt or shame about something. If you can blame someone else, then you don't have to help or take any responsibility for it. Also, if you can recruit someone else to demonize another with you, then you feel supported and you must be right if others agree with you. Another possible reason to join in with demonizers is to fit in with the "in" group who are the demonizers. If you do it openly in front of the person, then there is an element of bullying in it. Demonizing can be a very serious error, born of flaws in human nature, and courageous action is often needed to thwart it.

Project A Feeling Of Safety

If we want to communicate honestly with our colleagues, it helps to project a feeling of *safety*. They need to feel that it is safe to talk with us. One way to create safety and trust, at least in the beginning, is to talk about mutual self-interest: "I'm interested in your problem because it's my problem too."

It's easy to destroy a feeling of safety. All you have to do is criticize or threaten others, and they will be gone. It's better to be silent than to drive them away, unless the silence is perceived as threatening. If someone asks for confidentiality, then demonstrate your willingness to provide that, maybe by suggesting a safe and quiet meeting place. You could express understanding and point out that you know what it is like to need confidentiality. Or you could say that you know what it is like to be in that situation. You could also include in your response what you *don't* mean as well as what you *do* mean. For example, you could say that you *don't* mean that the other person is not doing his or her job, but only that it could appear that way.

Let's say that you respond to another with a sly smile, or with a moral judgment such as, "You shouldn't have done that. It is wrong." This will create fear and distrust in the other person. If your colleague sees you laughing about him or her with others, then it is all over for building trust. Whatever the reality of the situation, if you want to form good relationships with colleagues, then making them feel safe is a good way to begin. After you create this feeling and the other is opening up, it may be time to listen patiently. You can even offer criticisms without the other running away if you first create a feeling of safety.

In summary, communication is so powerful that several specific guidelines are worth following.

- Be gentle, positive, and uplifting.
- Project a feeling of safety in others.
- Use empathy and compassion rather than judgment and righteousness.
- Do not approve of inappropriate discussions about colleagues. Make it clear when you think something is hearsay or unproven.

- Do not let broad, negative comments about colleagues go unquestioned. They only encourage and unwittingly approve additional comments of that type. Avoid trash talk.
- Be careful of demonizing others. Even if guilty of wrongdoing, the person is still a human being. We all make mistakes.

The Golden Rule

The golden rule, which is to treat others as we would want to be treated, goes back to at least the seventh century BCE.[9] It is found perhaps in all cultures and is one of those obvious truths about collegial behavior. By itself, it can have a major, positive impact. The way it operates is relatively simple. Just put yourself in the shoes of someone you interact with, and ask yourself "How would I like to be treated?" It is a reciprocal consideration involving at least two people. It includes empathy, attempts at understanding others, and maybe action.

There is a difficulty with the golden rule, though. How do you know how the other person wants to be treated? There may be major cultural or perspective differences between you. You may not understand the other's position, and it may not be what it seems. Your interests and values may be different from those of the other person. Considered in this light, the golden rule has its limitations. Additional communication may be needed to find out how the other person wants to be treated. At least the golden rule brings a relatively clear standard to collegial behavior which is to avoid hurting others because no one, including you, likes to be hurt (this is the negative form of the rule). Because of the difficulty with the golden rule, the "platinum rule" has been developed, which is "treat others the way *they* want to be treated."[10] This helps us shift from what *I* want to what *others* want. It is a helpful shift of focus.

"First Do No Harm" Or Minimize Harm

Another useful guideline in dealing with colleagues probably derives from the Hippocratic Oath: first do no harm. Or perhaps a more realistic goal is to *minimize harm*. Consider the following case.

A new faculty member, Dr. Sharpe, is in a kind of trouble. He is outstanding in many ways: he is very successful, comes from a high-powered university, and is a recent "trophy" hire. But many of the other faculty members are critical of him, perhaps because he has been critical of their productivity. (It turns out that his boss, the director, has been critical of the same faculty members). They are beginning to harp on Dr. Sharpe's flaws, and negative rumors that he is overly judgmental and hostile are becoming vicious even though there is little evidence to support the rumors. Even though Dr. Sharpe has denied the truth of the rumors, they have hurt his reputation, and invitations for seminars and lectures have fallen off significantly. Dr. Sharpe has asked for support from colleagues and superiors, but it has not helped. Some members of the faculty and the administration think it would be best if he left the school.

The director who hired Dr. Sharpe is somewhat overwhelmed by the trouble and is not sure what to do. He does not think the rumors about his new hire are true, but he will not even admit that rumors exist when Dr. Sharpe asks about them. Nonetheless, it is clear to Dr. Sharpe that there are problems, perhaps serious ones. He repeatedly goes to his director for help and clarification without really getting any.

The director, who is new and not very experienced himself, has been thinking about his options. He has been urged by his superiors to find the courage to do *something*.

a) The director can ask Dr. Sharpe to leave. He could even get nasty about it. Maybe he could dig into Sharpe's past and reframe earlier problems in a negative way so that Sharpe is too embarrassed to stay. This seems easy, allows the director to largely ignore the problem, and shifts the burden to Sharpe. But some of the director's friends, more experienced administrators, point out that this will be harmful to Dr. Sharpe because it will appear to outsiders that he could not be defended and was undesirable.

b) He can try to get another department or school interested in Dr. Sharpe. The director knows many department heads throughout the country and considers calling them to say that Sharpe is available for hire. He actually does this with one chair but is met with suspicion and a blunt "no." The other chair has heard about the rumors and wants to know if they are true and if Sharpe is in real trouble. He wonders if the director is trying to pass on a problem to someone else. The director begins to realize that he may be hurting Sharpe by taking this option.

c) The director can explain the situation to Dr. Sharpe and work with him and his opponents toward a solution. This will take time and effort, but it will show that he has faith in Sharpe and that Sharpe still has value. But it will also mean that the director may have to stand up against those who want Sharpe out of the school. The director decides to announce that he plans to discuss this with Sharpe, find out the facts, and bring in professional helpers, if needed, to resolve the situation to everyone's satisfaction as best he can. Even though the director may be in some peril with this option, he feels that it is his responsibility.

The last option is obviously the collegial solution. Even though he may end up investigating Dr. Sharpe for bad behavior, it does give Sharpe the dignity and due process he deserves. It may be that Sharpe will decide to leave anyway, or perhaps everyone will be satisfied by a to-be-discovered solution. The director is to be congratulated for choosing to avoid the solutions that were easy but did harm to Dr. Sharpe. The guideline of doing no harm or minimizing harm may be especially useful when, for one reason or another, we don't know the facts and cannot easily discover them. You may turn this around and argue, with some validity, that life is not so simple. No matter what we do, we may harm someone in some way. If a situation does involve some harm no matter what, then minimizing harm is obviously the goal.

Detraction: The Evil Kind Of Truth

Can telling the truth ever be anti-collegial and harmful? Yes of course it can. Even if you tell "the truth" about someone, it can be damaging and inappropriate, especially if there is no need to do so. For example, if you reveal a person's faults or misdeeds from the past, without a valid reason, you are damaging their reputation. Some religious traditions refer to this as the sin of *detraction*.[11] Collegiality asks that you respect the reputation of persons and avoid words that will cause unjust injury. Everyone is allowed past mistakes and the opportunity to put misdeeds behind them. We, who have our own misdeeds, have no right to damage others. By bringing up past misdeeds we can destroy the reputation of others, even those who have worked incessantly to repair their previous errors. Sometimes detractors say, "Well, it's the truth isn't it?" But would we like it if our past errors were broadcast in a righteous manner as though we were evil? Compassion and empathy are major values in collegial ethics. In chapter 8, there is a case titled "Do we reveal the past?" that explores this topic further.

Developing Courage

In the previous chapter, courage was described as critical to getting involved. This chapter discusses how to develop it. We can consider different kinds of courage.[12] There is physical courage shown, for example, by firemen saving someone from a fire. There is intellectual courage shown by people like Galileo whose new ideas went against the ruling hierarchy. Then we have moral courage, which is to act in a way we believe to be right. It is possible to train yourself to be courageous, although the specific methods may be different and depend on the situation. Training for physical courage will involve physical training and mental discipline. A generally useful way to develop courage is to read about courageous men and women. Look at those who were in a situation similar to yours if possible. How did they handle it? Focus on the positive results of their actions. Obvious giants of moral courage include Winston Churchill, Mahatma Gandhi, and Martin Luther King Jr.

Courage can be practiced and developed in many small ways every day. Own up to things you have done, like getting ink on the carpet, even if it makes you look foolish. If someone charges you too little, speak up and pay the correct amount. Speak fairly and generously about others when you can, even if you are under pressure to do otherwise. This practice makes it easier when a highly challenging situation comes along. Courage is built one small step at a time. This approach allows you to face fears, small ones at first. It helps you see who you are and what your particular fears are. When you know your personal fears, you can confront them and find your way through them. As you do the things you fear, the fear will diminish.

A number of steps have been suggested for helping manage our fears, but you must "give a little time" to it.[13] One practice is called "reframing," which means changing the way you view a certain situation. Instead of repeating negative thoughts or thoughts about how you might be harmed, you can reframe them by looking at the benefits that could occur. Another practice is to confront the worst. For example, if you have been ruminating on a particular catastrophic event, you can calmly ask yourself, "What if it does happen? What are my responses to this?" The point is that you may be able to plan for and control negative outcomes. Another step is self-soothing or self-calming. You can take specific steps to calm yourself when facing a fearful situation. They could include venting to others, gathering support from others, meditating, journaling, exercising, or any other type of activity that is calming.

An important step is managing and accepting risk. We avoid risk for many of the reasons described in previous chapters. We are afraid of being hurt or of being embarrassed. But fear can be dealt with. Begin with being clear about the risk you may take. Ask yourself, what exactly am I risking? What is the worst thing that can happen, and can I live with it? But don't focus only on the danger. Identify clearly what you want to accomplish and what you have to do to achieve it. Ask yourself what are the barriers and what are my resources? What are the gains? *Focusing on the gains* is a productive approach. Supporting a colleague now may help prevent a situation later where you might be hurt.

The positive side of risk taking is that it can bring sizable rewards. By acting courageously, we can have a significant, positive impact on others. But we need to be prudent and aware of our own limitations. If we can't accept some worst-case scenarios, then perhaps it is better if someone else takes the risk. Some of these steps will be covered again in the chapters on developing collegial skills. Developing the skills required for taking supportive collegial actions requires time, effort, and thought, which should be included in training.

Consider the following case. You are a senior person in your organization, and a couple of younger people ask if they can speak to you about a private matter. They seem a little frightened, so you plan to meet them at a coffee shop, away from work. You meet them there, and you can see that they are hesitant to talk, but you encourage them and try to reduce their fear and produce a feeling of safety. You promise confidentiality. You tell them that many people speak to you confidentially about work, and there never has been a problem. You also tell them they don't have to mention names and that you won't know if it is related to work or not. Given these assurances, they slowly open up and tell you their concerns. Someone they know, call that person X, has been seriously wronged, and it has impacted X's life in a negative way. The problem is that they think they should tell X or someone in authority about it, and they want to, but they are worried that they will be dragged into a conflict and maybe get hurt. They are thinking that they should preserve their own safety first.

You ask, "How serious is the problem? Has someone broken the law?"

"We don't know for sure, but maybe that's happened."

"Well, then you may be required by law to come forward, but I'm not a lawyer so I can't say for sure even if I had all the details."

One of them says, "If we weren't so scared, we could probably think more clearly about it."

You say, "It is very wise that you are being careful. Whistle-blowers often get hurt, and they need to be careful about any action they take. It is a good thing that there are two of you because you can help each other think about it. Don't forget to think about the possible benefits of your actions. What's the best thing that can happen and how important is it? Have you thought about the worst thing that could happen? Can you tolerate that?"

"Well, we don't think much can happen to us. It is just frightening to go to authorities and report on somebody."

"Yes, that is true. But maybe you can be very careful about how you do this. Don't give your opinions about anything. What I mean is, tell what you have seen or heard. Then if you want, you can say what you think it means. Separate your data or observations from your interpretations of it. You can let someone else assess what it means. Is that helpful?"

They nod in unison. They say they will think about it and that they don't think it has to be done today; there is time.

They said they would consider my advice and thanked me.

A couple of weeks later, they asked if we could meet again at the same place. After settling in and ordering, one of them quickly said, "Well, it has been done and resolved. After our meeting, we talked with each other and with another friend. That gave us a good idea of what the options were, and we all decided that we would stick together no matter what happened. The mutual support we got from this helped with our courage. Reading and talking about historic people who were undecided, fearful but ultimately courageous also helped us. So we went to a person in charge and described our concerns exactly like you suggested. We told her what we saw, what we heard, and what we feared it might mean. That made it a lot easier and less scary. She informed us that she knew about the issue and that this new information could be very helpful. She congratulated us on how careful we were in the way we reported the problem.

"We were so relieved we suddenly felt exhilarated. It was an experience that we won't forget. Thank you so much for your help. Without your advice, we probably would not have come forward and would have probably regretted it. Thanks again."

You congratulate them on their good judgment and their courage. You don't know who X was or what was involved, but you are glad that you helped these younger colleagues resolve the conflict.

In another case, a worker received an e-mail about politics from a colleague. It was an unsettling e-mail because it spoke very unkindly about the president of our country and had other slurs in it as well. The worker was upset by the e-mail but continued normally through the day and went home that night. After thinking about it for some hours, the worker decided to reply to the sender of the email.

"I appreciate your thinking about me in your various activities, but I don't want to receive any more e-mails of that kind. I thought there were inappropriate slurs in it, and since when do we have so little respect for the office of the president of this country that we denigrate it so easily? I really don't want to be part of this network."

Well, the reply was an immediate apology and an admission that a couple of other people had responded the same way. In fact, more and more people seemed to be responding negatively to the comments. Showing some courage can catalyze other people to show their own courage and to respond in the same way. Just like negative comments can have an impact and spread like a virus, so does courage. That is one of the reasons that we need to stand up for what we think. Now only does it help us, it helps others find their courage as well. Acts of courage can open up parts of our lives. Anaïs Nin said that life shrinks or expands in proportion to one's courage.

Empathy and compassion, qualities that are emphasized in this book, are great helpers in taking courageous action. If you can empathize with people who are wronged, then you can help them more easily. If you rise up in life so that you become wealthy, and if you don't forget what it's like to be poor, then you can more readily stand up to your wealthy peers and help the less fortunate. Offering regular service to others who are more needy than you can broaden your experience, help develop compassion, and provide a moral basis for courage.

Courage does not mean damaging or seriously hurting yourself. Courage should be coupled with sound judgment and experience, as described in chapter 4. Appropriate courage is an asset not only in terms of ethics, but in many other ways throughout life.

Giving Credit To Others

One of the nicest things you can do for your colleagues is to give them credit for a job well done. "Hey, what a good job you did. We wouldn't be this far along without you." Or, "You managed that conflict beautifully. Everyone is happier now." Giving credit recognizes talent and hard work, and is sometimes the only reward your coworkers ever get. It shows your appreciation for their efforts.

Maybe you can nominate a colleague for an award or some other recognition. A letter to the boss about another's work can be powerful. Sometimes credit is taken by the supervisor for something done by a subordinate, and, to an extent, that seems appropriate when supervisors play a role in the success, so long as credit is also given precisely where it is due. Sometimes credit is due for an individual, courageous and an out-of-the-box achievement. Also, don't forget to give credit to the boss as well. Giving credit to those above you and to those below you in the hierarchy is a generous and nourishing act. You can include your own contributions so long as it doesn't sound like you are really giving yourself credit and not others.

What happens when you don't give credit? It might mean that a person is deprived of something that he/she is really due, which is an ethical issue. When people don't get credit for their work it creates morale problems which can affect health and productivity. Giving appropriate credit, either openly or in evaluations or by other means, is a highly collegial and supportive action. You will be remembered by your colleagues.

Mentoring Others

Mentoring is an almost sacred gift to others. Sadly, it is not always available or wanted. But a fact of life seems to be that others can see our folly more readily than we can. We can be so caught up in a problem, so emotional and distracted, that we may not be thinking of all the options. Just think how often a good friend makes a helpful suggestion. Mentoring by close friends or others has a high priority in collegial ethics. Like any element of our culture, collegial ethics will become embedded if mentoring and living the process of collegial ethics is done to a great enough degree and for a long enough time.

Acceptance as a mentor likely requires that the mentor is exemplary in collegiality—that is, he or she practices what they preach.

Also, mentoring can take some skill. Some people have a knack for making mentoring look easy, and others have to work at it. But it is well worth the effort if you can help others.

Suppose you see a young colleague loudly complaining about another and looking very frustrated:

"She drives me crazy. I can't stand it."

"What's the problem?" you ask.

"She is never on time for meetings."

"Never?" you say, adding that that would make you unhappy also.

"Well, not today."

You call the colleague aside, and in a private place you suggest that he keep his cool. You point out that supervisors and colleagues can be turned off by people who lose their cool. You also mention that it is OK to vent under certain conditions, but that you need to be more careful.

You give your colleague some examples of how to handle the situation. You tell him, "You might say, 'She was late today even though I reminded her. It makes me frustrated because I'm really busy today.' That seems more in control and more reasonable. Also, saying it that way lets you take responsibility for your reactions."

You keep the situation in mind and look for an opportunity to chat with the woman who has frustrated your colleague.

In another situation, almost identical to the one described in chapter 1, you come across a colleague looking very thoughtful and worried. You ask what's on her mind, and she blurts out "I think Tom is cheating. I think he's making up data." She is clearly very distressed.

"What did you see?"

"I saw him watching the data monitor and writing down numbers in his notebook that were different from the numbers on his monitor."

"Did you ask what exactly he was doing?"

"No, I should have, but I was so shocked I was speechless."

As you look into the situation further, you find out that Tom was subtracting in his mind a background value from the data and writing down the result. The background would have to be subtracted anyway. So there was no wrongdoing.

You let the worried colleague know what you found, and she lets out a sigh of relief.

"Did you tell anyone else you thought he was doing something wrong?"

"No, I didn't because you stepped in and said you would look into it. I'm glad you did. I almost made a big mistake."

"Yes. *Just remember to separate in your mind what you see from what you think it means.* There could be many reasons for what you see, and be sure not to jump to conclusions that might be harmful to others." Together you talk about that last point, and she seems like she has a new way of looking at such issues. The two of you part closer and friendlier.

Sometimes mentors are especially valuable because of their experience and restraint in judgment. Sometime younger colleagues fully believe sweeping generalizations and what we call "urban myths." This can be particularly dangerous. For example, some feel that they can't change their behavior. A great excuse is that "I can't change. My father was the same way. We just don't think of others. It's not in our genes." While it is true that our family and genetics *influence* our behavior, they do not fully *determine* our behavior (except in some special rare, diseases perhaps). Psychologists and geneticists who have examined the genetic basis of behavior find that although particular genes can be associated with certain behaviors or mental illnesses they don't *fully* cause them. In other words, it's not simple. One example is that one member of an identical twin pair can have a mental illness, while the other doesn't. So genetics are not the sole influence on us even for serious diseases. Having genes associated with certain behaviors may make us more likely to do them, but they are very *unlikely to force* us to behave in any particular way. We can change the way we are. We can alter our habits and preferences. Some may find this more difficult than others, depending on the change undertaken. Consider the following case.

Sharon, a recent hire, has a good record and is doing a good job. She works hard and tries to please everyone. Some of her colleagues, including Debra, don't like her, and Debra finds out that Sharon's family of origin does not have a good reputation. Her father spent time in jail (albeit for a misdemeanor), and her sister has been called a troublemaker. Debra broadcasts the negative information about Sharon's family and says that Sharon has "bad blood" and is "no good." Debra tells you this also—she seems to feel that she is obligated to tell you. You wonder if Debra's dislike of Sharon influences her actions and opinions. You might decide to try to mentor Debra and Sharon and you begin to analyze the situation.

1. Does Debra's dislike of Sharon create problems here? Is simply *disliking* someone a justifiable reason for discriminating against them at the *professional* level?

2. What does collegiality say about dredging up someone's past? Detraction is discussed above in this chapter.

3. What do you think about Debra? What do you tell her? How do you question the basis for her position? What do you think about her using the phrases "bad blood" and "no good"?

4. What about the genetics of behavior? Do our genes "influence" or do they "determine" our behavior? Do our parents influence or determine our behavior? This may require some research. Should Sharon be concerned about her future behavior?

A justifiable and scientifically based position is that genetics does influence our behavior, but does not totally determine it. In studies of violence, for example, biological factors account for only about 50 percent of the variance in becoming violent. Many or most people with genetic vulnerabilities do not become violent. Genetics are an influence but not a life sentence. Even identical twins, who start out in the womb with the same genetic makeup, are born with some differences in gene structure and their output due to different mutations and errors within the cells of the growing body. Even in genetically identical twins, fingerprints, irises, body scents and personalities are different.[14] The bottom line is that genetics influences our behavior but is not the whole story. It is important to realize that the environment has a major influence on genetic expression—a process described as *epigenetics,* which you can research as well. No one experiences the environment in exactly the same way, and hence their epigenetic changes will vary. We are the product of our genetic heritage, our experiences, and our environment.

Having thought about all this, you put together a plan to work with both Debra and Sharon so that they are more informed about genetics and behavior and the others questions that have come up. They need the facts. As a mentor, you can do a great deal of good for these colleagues.

Collegial Ethics and The Boss

Ranked and hierarchical relationships have problems of their own when it comes to ethics and behavior. What is in the best interest of the employee, for example, may not always be in the best interest of the employer. When best interests coincide, that is ideal. When they don't, there may be thorny problems.

Why should we support the boss? There are many good reasons, in general. For example, we need to keep in mind that it's not always easy being the boss. Bosses can be very different, as we know, and sometimes they are hired because they are different from their predecessor or from other supervisors. But we need to let each boss do it his own way, so long as he doesn't deviate from accepted practices. We owe it to our superiors to allow them to have unique personalities—just like we do—and to do it their way. One supervisor might prefer lots of small group meetings; another might want fewer but larger meetings. One might be personable and remember everyone's name, while another might not. We could imagine hundreds of differences between two possible supervisors.

What happens when a boss is destructive to you? If you aren't doing well, you can't expect to be praised or even kept on if the problems are big enough. On the other hand, if you are treated unfairly, then you have the right to speak up. In many states employees have relatively few working rights. In others, they may have more. If you are in a union, you may be able to get help more easily. Depending on the situation, you could always consult a labor lawyer.

Bosses have an imperative not only to ensure productivity but to be fair as well—at least as fair as they can be, given their commitment to the company or institution. What we see as fair may not be fair to someone else who has other demands and expectations. If the company changes and you don't, then you may be in jeopardy because the boss may be there to produce change. While it is complicated, bosses are nevertheless expected to be collegial in their way, especially if you are giving them what they want. This issue is discussed from a different perspective and in greater detail in chapter 7 in a section on hierarchical issues.

The Bottom Line

There are effective ways to present and teach collegial ethics. They involve: a) gathering guidelines, cases, and courses, b) forming discussion groups, role-play groups, and c) developing mentors. There are several important topics to address. Because language is so powerful, how we talk to others requires careful scrutiny. A benign, neutral or supportive style of communicating seems essential. Be positive, uplifting and safe. Useful guidelines include "do no harm," or at least "minimize harm," as well as the golden and platinum rules. A key factor is courage; without it we might not be able to do great good. Ranked and hierarchical relationships can pose complications for collegial ethics; both the higher and lower ranked individuals have to respect each other, and both have their own responsibilities. Giving credit to colleagues for a job well done is a highly collegial and nourishing act. Mentoring is a needed skill because many find person to person learning with its immediate feedback more efficient and easier than advice from a text.

Notes for Chapter 5

1. Mark Twain, attribution, http://www.citehr.com/41401-famous quotes-training-development.html#ixzz20Ws56hb4, accessed July 1, 2012.

2. Lewis Carroll http://www.values.com/inspirational-quotes/value/25-Helping-Others/, accessed July 1, 2012.

3. For example, see http://www.uth.tmc.edu/orsc/training/ResearchMisconduct/index.htm, accessed March 21, 2012.

4. http://stress.about.com/od/positiveattitude/qt/helping.htm, accessed July 30, 2012.

5. http://www.helpothers.org/. http://zenhabits.net/25-ways-to-help-a-fellow-human-being-today/, accessed July 30, 2012.

6. http://www.mendosa.com/snow.html, accessed June 26, 2012.

7. M. B. Rosenberg, *Nonviolent Communication: A Language of Life* (Encinitas CA: Puddledancer Press, 2003).

8. From M. J. Kuhar, "Collegial Ethics: What Why and How," *Drug and Alcohol Dependence* no. 119 (2011): 235–238.

9. D. D. Runes, *Pictorial History of Philosophy* (New York: Philosophical Library, 1959).

10. See http://www.alessandra.com/abouttony/aboutpr.asp or http://www.platinumrule.com/index.html, accessed August 15, 2012.

11. For example, see *Catechism of the Catholic Church*, Paulist Press, Mahwah NJ, 1994

12. http://artofmanliness.com/2009/02/08/developing-manly-courage/, accessed July 26, 2012.

13. V. D. Lachman, "Strategies Necessary for Moral Courage," *The Online Journal of Issues in Nursing* 15 no. 3, manuscript 3 (2010).

14. Williams C, "One and Only You," *New Scientist*, July 28, 2012, 32–36.

6

Collegial Skills: Feelings and Needs

> *Language is a tool adequate to provide any degree of*
> *precision relevant to a particular situation.*
> — Kenneth L. Pike[1]
>
> *Once we feel our emotions and needs have been heard,*
> *there's often a sense of relief and release. Then we can*
> *move on to finding the best strategy for meeting the*
> *identified need.*
> —Sandra Pawula[2]

This chapter summarizes some existing approaches that focus on expressing feelings and needs and resolving conflicts. These approaches are included here because of the importance of communicating with and resolving conflict with our colleagues. While the approaches are somewhat different, they are complementary and can greatly help our intercollegial interactions.

Nonviolent Communication (NVC)

Nonviolent communication (NVC) is a process developed by Marshall Rosenberg, PhD, who was trained as a clinical psychologist. He views NVC as a process in which compassion and empathy flow positively and constructively between people. Anti-NVC processes include moralistic judgments, comparisons, and denials of responsibility. NVC is a procedure for avoiding violence, even subtle forms, and for promoting peaceful cooperation and a search for understanding and solutions. No effort will be made to cover the entire subject, but more comprehensive information is available.[3]

Improving Communication

The importance of words in communication has been stressed previously, and a mastery of words is important. Ruth Bebermeyer wrote a poem in which she says that words can be like windows or they can be like walls.[3] How true. The exact words we use, the way we use them, and the emotions we feel when we use them have a great impact on how our communication is received.

There are four major components of NVC: observations, feelings, needs, and requests. Utilizing these components helps us connect with each other in a way that allows us to communicate well and to see each other's needs. Seeing each other's needs cuts through rhetoric and points out the real issues. Some people use NVC to create a greater depth in interpersonal relationships or to build stronger collegial relationships. NVC can be used to mediate disputes and conflicts, and it is obviously something that can help us in our goal of behaving more collegially.

When someone addresses us, we employ NVC by *listening* carefully to the words and then trying to grasp the *feelings and needs* hidden behind them. Suppose your wife approaches you and says, "I wish you wouldn't spend so much time at work." What she wants, but unfortunately is not very clear about, is more time together. If you are searching her words for her own personal needs, you might ask "Why?" and so forth, and figure it out. But if her needs never enter your mind, you might carry out her request and then announce that you are joining a bridge group that plays one or two nights a week.

It satisfies her verbal request, but not her unspoken need. While this scenario is hypothetical, it clearly shows the general problem. Empathy, which is discussed further below, is part of listening, particularly when the communicator is distressed.

Conversely, when we address others, we try to express our own observations, feelings, and needs, and, if necessary, make appropriate requests. When someone is doing something you don't like, for example, like looking over your shoulder at your private work, instead of becoming angry and saying to your colleague, "Why don't you go and do something else?" you might use NVC communication.

You might say, "Would you please not look over my shoulder at my work? It makes me self-conscious and slows me down."

An appropriate, direct response back to you might be, "I'm sorry, I just wasn't thinking." That reply would be more suitable instead of a sarcastic response like, "Well aren't you so very important." The wife requesting that her husband work less should have said, "I'm feeling a little lonely in the evenings, and I want to spend more time together. Can we find a way to spend two nights a week by ourselves?"

Consider another situation. Supposing you come across a colleague, Ray, who is fuming with anger. He says, "Fred over there really upsets me. He seems to be running to the boss with my ideas all the time. I've been giving him dirty looks, and I swear at him when I pass his desk, but he just hasn't gotten the idea. He continues to go to the boss with my ideas and makes it look like they are his."

Here is an opportunity for mentoring. You realize how not giving proper credit can be demoralizing. You might say "Ray, have you told him directly what your feelings and needs are?" You could coach Ray so that his responses, needs, and feelings are clear, and you could also encourage him to state clearly what he wants from Fred.

He might say, "Fred, I've been upset. I feel like you go to the boss with my ideas, which makes me feel that you have no respect for me as a colleague. I'm just like everyone else, and I need to have my contributions recognized. Maybe because of your enthusiasm for this work, you aren't aware of what you are doing to me. I was hoping that you would not do this anymore, or at least give me the opportunity to talk to the boss about my own ideas. At the very least I feel you should give me the credit I need when you talk to him." No matter what the response of the colleague might be, it is clear that this kind of expression is much more informative. It states what's happening, describes your feelings, presents your needs, and makes a specific request. The colleague might come back and say that he was sorry, or he may have information that shows you are not entirely correct. If both colleagues use the four components of NVC, they are more likely to reach a mutual understanding. Of course, all of this should be said in a very sincere way. Saying these things by yelling or belittling your colleague in front of others can only make the situation worse.

If anti-NVC approaches are used, understanding is much less likely. Suppose you encouraged Ray to approach Fred and use a moralistic judgment. Ray might publicly call him a "sneaking thief"! This is much less likely to help solve the problem, unless Fred caves in and apologizes; even then, he might also hold a secret grudge. In any case, Fred still won't know what Ray's feelings and needs are.

Another anti-NVC approach would be to say, "Wouldn't so and so be more aggressive and straighten Fred out? Be more like so and so. You are acting like a wimp." Making such a comparison with so and so is less helpful because it misdirects the issues from what your colleague really needs, which is credit for his own ideas, to acting like someone else would. Now that could be perfectly appropriate, but it is a little risky. In addition to not being as direct as possible, comparisons can block our compassion, cause us to lose confidence, and leave us miserable.

Sometimes people won't share their concerns with you for various reasons. Perhaps they are afraid, or perhaps they don't really want to work out some problem. This lack of communication will likely leave you both dead in the water. It is difficult at best to resolve anything when you are kept in the dark or lied to.

Responsibility

Taking responsibility for our feelings and reactions to others is a cornerstone of NVC. Suppose a colleague snipes at you by saying, "Boy, you really kiss up to the boss, don't you?" In response, you can feel guilty and blame yourself, or you can feel insulted and blame the sniping colleague. You could also respond by calmly explaining your feelings and needs.

You could say, "When you accuse me like that, I feel attacked, and I'm not even sure exactly what you are objecting to. When I interact with the boss, I'm only trying to get my ideas across in a tactful way and hope that my ideas will be useful to him."

Yet another approach would be to focus on the feelings and needs of the sniping and grumbling colleague. You could reply, "Oh, are you feeling that the boss doesn't pay any attention to you? Can I help you get your ideas across to him?" Considering feeling and needs in our interactions—in spite of hostile and provocative communications—improves communication and increases the chance of a positive and helpful outcome.

Another issue is thinking that the comments and actions of others *cause* your inner responses, such as anger, frustration, envy, or whatever. In the previous example, when the colleague says, "You really kiss up to the boss, don't you?" you could get furiously angry and blame the colleague for *causing* your anger. But NVC doesn't sanction this. We become fully responsible when we accept our own selves, not someone else, as responsible for our reactions. They may be a stimulus, but we, not they, *choose* our own reactions, and we need to accept responsibility for our feelings. In response to the comment about kissing up to the boss, instead of getting angry, you can take a minute and ask yourself if you should choose to be angry or to respond in another way—it is your *choice*. (Note that this position is not exactly the same as the one proposed by collegial ethics. Collegial ethics promotes the idea that we have responsibility for the impact of our actions and words on others. Nevertheless, this does not rule out choosing among our possible reactions). You can see how important these skills are for communicating calmly and effectively with others, which was also discussed in chapter 5.

There are many speech patterns or selections of words that reveal when we aren't taking full responsibility for our actions. One is to use "we" instead of "I." "*We* think you are a mess" vs. "*I* think you are having a hard time because I think your grades are going down." "*We* have been angry at you" vs. "*I* have been angry with you because I feel you snubbed me." If we try to use a pattern where we say "I feel… because I…," we will be more true to ourselves, and it will help us experience our own responsibility for our reactions and feelings. This can have a big impact on us as well as on our colleagues. Are you in the habit of taking responsibility for your comments and feelings?

An anti-NVC approach is to deny responsibility for our feelings and actions. "You made me do it." Or "I was told to do it," or "I take illegal drugs because everyone else in my group does." In the last example, it sounds like the group has power over the speaker's behavior. A more responsible statement might be, "I take drugs because I choose too, in spite of the risks." Instead of saying, "I go to work because I have to," you could say, "I go to work because I want the paycheck and a secure future." Other honest motives and reasons include acting to get approval, to escape punishment, to avoid guilt and shame, or maybe to satisfy a sense of duty. Using language and a choice of words that lets us express responsibility for our actions helps us see our situation in a realistic light, and also helps us realize that we may have the power to make changes in our lives if we choose to.

Separate What You See From What You Think

A great many messes have been made by mixing observations with evaluations or conclusions. The case of Students X and Z in chapter 1 shows this, where Student Z thought Student X was making up data (and said so), but what he really observed was that Student X was writing down numbers different from those on the computer screen, and it turned out that there was a good reason for this. We mix up observations and conclusions in many ways.

We might say that, "Ted is not a good worker." But a more accurate statement might be, "Ted has not met his production or sales quota in three months." Or we might say, "Grace is antisocial." But that would be better stated as, "Grace has left the last two office parties early and didn't seem to want to talk to me." We owe it to each other to be concrete in what we say rather than make overstated judgments that can be damaging and alienating to others.

A major part of NVC is avoiding vague communications that are confusing or ambiguous. Being clear about feelings and needs and making requests for ourselves must be done while taking full responsibility for our own actions and reactions. If you want to be sure that a colleague understands what you are saying, you can ask for feedback or a simple restatement of what you said or did. Why waste time? Communicate effectively and clearly and talk about what you feel and need. But as stated earlier in this book, watch out for inappropriate and alienating feelings that will drive you and your colleagues apart.

Using Empathy

Empathy is being sensitive to and aware of others and their feelings. It is not judging or fixing their problem. It is simply experiencing their feelings and emotions, and it can make others feel like they are understood and heard. It can relieve anger, heal, and move us on to a solution. This powerful process doesn't require you to do much. You simply have to open your mind and listen non-judgmentally. But it may not be simple, and it may require practice. After empathizing, you can then develop a feel for the needs of another and go from there. This amazing and powerful process requires taking some time to listen to the other person and finding a way to signal understanding.

NVC Summary

To summarize, NVC is a process in which we take time for empathetic and compassionate listening. Major components of the process include expressing observations, feelings, needs, and requests. These components can be used to structure your communications for improved clarity and effectiveness. Separate what you objectively see from what you subjectively think or feel. Taking responsibility for our actions and feelings is important; using statements like "I feel… because I…" is helpful. We, not others, are responsible for our own feelings and reactions; others do not cause our reactions—we can choose our reactions to others. Using empathy can create a caring attitude. These guidelines and practices can make communication more effective and useful.

Conflict Resolution (CR)

Conflict is a part of our daily lives. It is part of collegial interactions, and how we deal with it will determine the outcome of many of those collegial interactions. It occurs because we are all different, live in different conditions, and have different wants and needs. If we have a need or a special interest in some object, conflict can arise if another wants it (or takes it). Relationships can spawn conflict—as everyone has experienced—and a values clash can create conflict. Moreover, there can be structural or hierarchical conflicts when there are unequal distributions of resources, power, or authority. Conflicts can arise in many ways, and we need to be able to handle them.

Some of us deal with conflict quite well, while others run from it and don't handle it. When conflict isn't dealt with, it might be OK to ignore it, but it might also lead to continued and unresolved problems that could escalate. Conflict can be stressful, and stress can be bad not only for your relationships but also for your health. Conflict in groups and among colleagues could become toxic, leading to a functional collapse of the group. Fortunately, many people have thought about conflict and how to resolve it. [4-9] Because conflict affects collegial interactions and can severely impair them, conflict resolution (CR) is an important skill for satisfying our own needs and those of others. A study of the communication styles when couples fight and argue showed that certain styles were predictive of divorce. Negative outcome styles include avoiding the issues so that nothing gets worked out, being disrespectful and criticizing the other person's character, or avoiding discussion of specific problems.[10, 11] CR skills can be a huge asset as you negotiate your way in life.

Let us take the view that conflict is *normal, natural, neutral, and even necessary.* That is a lot to say, and it may take a while to let it sink in. Conflict in and of itself is not good or bad; it is neutral and there is no reason to struggle with that view. Because of our real and normal differences, conflict is normal, and because we have to get our needs met, conflict is very often necessary. Conflict is going to happen, so there is no reason to get tense about it. Prepare yourself instead. We have the skills available to us to resolve it if we choose to learn and use them. Resolutions of conflicts occur every day in thousands of settings, so it can be done. Some conflicts do seem to go on forever, and some lead to a lot of destruction; this is all the more reason to learn CR. The more you learn about how to handle conflict, the less you will run from it and struggle with it, and the more naturally you'll be able to handle difficult colleagues and difficult situations.

Win-Win Strategies

One of the core strategies of CR is win-win. It means just what it sounds like: both you and your colleague (or everyone involved in the conflict) win. If both of you win, then that is a solution both of you can accept. It's done. But finding the win-win position can take effort. A commitment of time is essential to work it all out. It may require soul-searching or analyzing each other's positions. It will require you to examine your *needs*—not only your *wants* but your true needs. It may help you to go even further and empathize with each other and show compassion for each other. Turning the problem around and around, discussing each other's perspective, and seeing the good in the other's needs will hopefully lead to a suitable solution sooner or later. A suitable solution will meet at least some of each person's needs. Getting to win-win is what training in CR is about.

Responses To Conflict

Before we go further, we need to review how each of us responds to conflict. We need to do this if only to understand that there are many ways to respond.

Some of us use a *competitive* style. This means that we maintain our desire to win, and we continue to search, even struggle, to find a way to *win*. In this approach, the other's needs are disregarded and your competitive style or effort to win dominates. You may feel that you are in the right and can't compromise in any way. This approach may, of course, result in a victory in the short run, but you will have made no progress in joining with your opponent or partner to find mutually agreeable and winning solutions.

Another style is *accommodating*. This is the opposite of competing because an individual ignores his or her own concerns and needs and allows the other person to satisfy his or her wants and needs. There is an element of self-sacrifice in this approach. It may be that it's simply not worth it to you to make an effort, so you let the other side win. It is also a form of generosity, which may in some situations be beneficial. But being accommodating means not being very assertive and you may end up not satisfying your own needs.

A third approach is *avoiding* conflict. This means walking away from it. It may be that the issues aren't very important to you or that the other party is insignificant to you. Hopefully it is not because you lack the skill or the will to deal with it. The problem with being avoidant is that the issues in the conflict are not addressed. It is not assertive nor is it cooperative. It is possible that this approach can be used to stall and wait for a better time or setting to deal with the problem.

Another way to approach conflict is referred to as *collaborating*. It is the opposite of avoiding the conflict and involves an attempt to work with the other to find a win-win solution, a solution that includes at least some of everyone's needs. It can be time-consuming, but it could be a good choice for those who need to work together even though there may be significant differences among the groups. If you really have to work together to reach a solution—for example, how to avoid a war—then continued collaboration is very important.

A final approach to conflict resolution is *compromising*. This comes in when neither side is able to reach an ultimate and totally satisfactory resolution to the conflict. Compromising aims at finding some mutually acceptable solution that may not be perfect for all but at least partially satisfies both parties. It may fall in the middle ground, and it may be considered a temporary solution until other, more long-term solutions can be found. Compromising usually means something like splitting the difference, seeking a middle ground, or giving up one requirement if the opponents will do the same.

Of these five styles or strategies, it seems that collaborating and compromising are the approaches that most often come into play in situations where the stakes are high for each side. They may also take the most energy and skill. But the other approaches can have benefits as well. If you are competing with someone over what you want, and you are getting nowhere, you can switch to another style, such as compromising. If you have been accommodating or giving into others and you find yourself angry and resentful, you can switch to a more collaborative and assertive position in the future. No one style is right or wrong, but which one we use will depend on the situation and the people. While each of us may have a favored style, we can learn how to apply different styles depending on the situation. Which styles are you using in the situations in your life? Could you benefit from changing styles?

Communicating In CR—Right Ways and Wrong Ways

The process of CR depends on communication. This means using both words and behavior, since behavior (our body language and expressions) is also a language in itself. Good communication in CR seeks to clarify what people need and want. "Please tell me what you want and why you want it. What will it do for you? To be sure I understand, let me say in my own words what I think you are saying."

If you are in a situation where someone wants what you have (and you want it too), you can say "I need it because…, and why do you need it?" If it's a complex situation with many issues, you can make progress by writing down what you do agree on and what you don't. What is essential for you, and what can each of you give up? "How can we both be happy?" is the essence of CR. If you are ready to give up things to get a solution, then the odds that it will work out increase.

We also have responses that do not work and make things worse. If someone wants something you have, and you say, "Take it, I don't care" when you really do care, that is a formula for frustration and tense relations. Perhaps you are embarrassed that you have it and feel you don't deserve it, or perhaps you don't know how to resolve such a small conflict and you avoid the whole process—to your own detriment.

A bad way to begin a confrontation is by criticizing another's character. "You always want what I have. You're greedy and never satisfied." This makes the discussion very vague (using always and never) and likely to produce a defensive response. It also does nothing to state what you want or need, and it does nothing to explore the other's wants or needs. It is a deadly opening statement. It is not only useless—it is a negative communication.

Another important aspect of good communication is to listen, listen, and listen. If you don't clearly hear what the other says, you will find it difficult to continue effectively. Maybe you should wait before formulating a response, even if it's just a few minutes. That time can be spent clarifying your thoughts and reactions, reflecting on the other person, finding empathy by putting yourself in the other's shoes, and just being sure you fully understand the request or comment. *Then* you can formulate a response to the issue. This process is not easy for some and requires practice. You can practice by role-playing with others and observing their behaviors and getting feedback on yours. Or you can use a video recorder to watch yourself and how you handle attacks or requests—this really is helpful if you can get past the self-conscious interest in how you look.

In order to communicate and get what you want, being assertive can be important. Assertiveness can be learned, and there are classes and programs that will help. One kind of assertiveness is to persist in communicating using "I need and feel…" statement rather than statements that are critical of others. Like the other skills discussed in this book, this can serve you well throughout your entire life.

Another somewhat ancillary but important CR skill is to know yourself, your feelings, your styles, and your needs. This is not always simple, and many of us don't have this knowledge. We can feel angry or uncomfortable without being clear on why we feel that way. Knowing ourselves can be a lifelong effort. Working with understanding and trusted friends or a psychotherapist can be helpful. If you know yourself and your needs, you'll know when your efforts with another are failing. When negotiation isn't working, you need to change your approach.

Sometimes getting help to resolve conflicts is the only way to move ahead. Consider a husband and wife with two children who are having a bitter argument. While they are lovers and parents, they are also colleagues in the sense that they work together to keep the family functioning and everyone growing and happy. The husband plays poker after work two nights a week, and the wife, who also has a job, wants him home more. She feels that most of the housework falls to her, and she wants help with the children and the house. She's exhausted and resentful, and she's been thinking about getting a divorce.

The husband feels that his wife is a complainer and that he does help out. She's so resentful, angry, and unpleasant that he says he'd play poker every night if it would get him away from her. They are hopelessly lost in the argument, calling each other names like *lazy* and *screamer*, and they end it by going in opposite directions, slamming a door, and fuming in private. This argument has happened before, and it is becoming more frequent.

Neither the husband nor the wife knows what to do. Neither of them had parents who solved problems well. Each one usually gave in to the other and were very accommodating in their style of conflict. It didn't work well because they were resentful and seemed to be hung up on the same problems for a long time. Just like her mother, the wife used to give in to her husband's wishes regularly, particularly when they were first married. But, now she was tired, bored with her life and marriage, fed up with being ignored, and angry and depressed. The husband felt harangued, angry, and confused about what to do. He just wanted to be away. He seemed to have the same problems at work from time to time and almost lost his job once or twice for continually arguing with other employees.

Desperate for options and help, the couple employed a family therapist. After listening to the couple, the therapist decided on a plan of action. In individual sessions, the therapist helped them draw up a list of complaints, and a few of them were easily solved. But the problem seemed to be more of an inability to deal with conflict. Training in CR was needed, since neither of them had models or mentors in CR.

First, the therapist worked with them to instill the idea that conflict was not bad but instead that it was to be expected and that it was in fact a "creative" opportunity to find a way to function better in everyday life. If they didn't have conflict in their marriage, it wouldn't be a marriage, and maybe it would be too late for them as a couple. Second, the therapist had to show them that they needed to change their style of arguing and resolving issues. There were more options than either giving in or withdrawing. The couple was quite interested in the latter point and even got a little enthusiastic when the therapist described other styles, such as collaborating on problem solving and compromising. Third, the couple was told that they had to stop certain ways of fighting. They had to stop calling each other names and making judgments about each other. They kept a log of their arguments, and they gradually learned to identify and stop negative communications. They also set aside some time every evening at first to discuss their problems.

After a couple of months, they were doing much better. While still wary of conflict, they didn't run from it any more. When they couldn't solve an issue, they wrote it down and kept working on it until it gave way to a solution. They tried to make it like a game, seeing who could come up with the most options. They worked on every complaint on the list compiled by the therapist, and they solved many of them. They learned to compromise on many issues. For example, the husband now played poker only one night per week, and the couple had a night out together on another night each week. They shopped together, and the husband agreed to take responsibility for keeping the family room in the house clean and orderly. He also agreed to take the children for a few hours each weekend so that the wife had some free time to herself. The husband was now much happier and wasn't defensive all the time. He had more quality time with his friends and coworkers. The wife was greatly relieved, stopped fantasizing about divorce, and wasn't angry and exhausted much of the time. Their marriage went from a horror show to a reasonable and caring relationship. Both had won something. They sometimes slid backward and reverted to old dysfunctional ways, but they were able, because of their new and helpful experiences, to pull themselves back on track. They found that as long as they were able to devote enough time to the issues, they did better and better.

The husband gradually began using his new skills at work. CR was becoming a habit. He calmly faced problems and conflicts as though they were natural, which they were. Just this one thing improved his functioning with his colleagues. He showed them how to collaborate on problem and solutions, and he was a model of direct and useful communication. After some time, the husband was promoted because he dealt with his colleagues so well that they grew to like and respect him.

Values Differences In CR

A core cause of conflict is a difference in values and worldview. There are many conflicts in society, for example, between the political right and left, between the religious and the secular, and between parents and teenagers. The problems can be minimal, but sometimes they are at the core of potentially destructive and troubling conflict. Worldview is how we view the world with our basic beliefs. Our worldviews can be very different. An example is the difference between someone who grew up in a strict religious environment, and someone who grew up in a nonreligious environment. In addition, the differences between a businessman whose goal is to make money and a philanthropist who wants to give it away are substantial. Differences in values and worldview can be at the core of many conflicts and can be the most difficult to deal with. A careful, thoughtful analysis of the underlying factors in conflict is required before taking a course of action. These situations can be among the most challenging.

CR Summary

Conflict is a fact of life and is normal, natural, neutral, and even necessary. It occurs because we are different and have different values, wants, and needs. Our responses to conflict vary and are sometimes habitual, but there are several styles that can be utilized. Certain styles of communication can be helpful and others can make conflict worse. A core strategy of CR is finding a win-win solution in which everyone gets some benefit.

Other Approaches

There are other approaches that contribute ideas to collegial ethics. Many of these have evolved as answers to international problems and include peacemaking and peace building. Peacemaking includes skills used to stall and eliminate conflict, while peace building is an effort that precedes possible conflict and builds peaceful approaches into a culture. One approach to peace building[12] relies on a process that includes analysis of the situation, a judgment on how best to proceed, avoidance of doing harm, intervention, and teaching or mentoring values that promote peace. It aims at reconciliation, justice, and conflict transformation. These skills are important in collegial ethics. Also, collegial ethics, like peace building, is proactive and intends to provide the skills to build a collegial environment and the skills to resolve conflict as it occurs. There are many groups, organizations, and approaches that have something to offer proponents of collegial ethics.

The Bottom Line

Over the years, many procedures have been developed to improve communication and to deal with conflict. These procedures utilize principles and ideas that can be a significant help in collegial ethics. The goal of collegial ethics is to support and help our colleagues, and conflicts are often at the core of collegial problems. Skill in resolving conflicts can be a great help.

NVC includes a group of skills and practices that facilitate clear and effective communication. It describes productive styles of communication as well as detrimental ones. Key elements of useful communication include stating observations, feelings, needs and requests. When we talk about a situation, we need to separate what we see from what we think it means. NVC urges that we take responsibility for our responses and reactions to others, rather than blame others.

Conflict is normal and even necessary at times; therefore learning to deal with it is essential. CR reduces the fear of conflict and describes many styles of handling it. It points out that communication can be effective and helpful, but inappropriate communications can make things worse; an emphasis on effective communication styles is important. A core goal is to find a win-win solution in which everyone involved gets something.

Both NVC and CR have goals that offer something for collegial ethics. NVC seems to focus more on communication, while CR focuses more on solving conflicts. Both stress how communication is key in relationships.

Notes for Chapter 6

1. Kenneth L. Pike, http://www.brainyquote.com/quotes/keywords/language_11.html#LIYRxpHpU0UbUyvY.99, accessed July 13, 2012.

2. Sandra Pawula, http://alwayswellwithin.com/2011/11/09/non-violent-communication/, accessed August 15, 2012.

3. M. B. Rosenberg, *Nonviolent Communication: A Language of Life* (Encinitas CA: Puddledancer Press, 2003).

4. http://www.conflictresolution.org/ and http://www.ehow.com/list_5955711_five-approaches-conflict.html, accessed July 2, 2012.

5. Arbinger Institute, *The Anatomy of Peace: Resolving the Heart of Conflict* (San Francisco: Berrett-Koehler, 2006).

6. R. Bolton, *People Skills: How to Assert Yourself, Listen to Others, and Resolve Conflicts* (New York: Simon and Schuster, 1979).

7. C. W. Moore, *The Mediation Process: Practical Strategies for Resolving Conflict* (San Francisco: Jossey-Bass, 2006).

8. D. R. Forsyth, *Group Dynamics,* 5th ed. (Pacific Grove, CA: Brooks/Cole, 2009).

9. J. H. Goldfie, and J. K. Robbennolt, "What If the Lawyers Have Their Way? An Empirical Assessment of Conflict Strategies and Attitudes toward Mediation Styles," *Ohio State Journal on Dispute Resolution* 22 (2007): 277–320.

10. J. M. Gottman, and S. Carrere, "Predicting Divorce among Newlyweds from the First Three Minutes of a Marital Conflict Discussion," *Family Process* 38 (1999): 293–301..

11. L. S. Matthews, K. A. S. Wickrama, and R. D. Conger. "Predicting Marital Instability from Spouse and Observer Reports of Marital Interaction," *Journal of Marriage and the Family* **58** (1996): 641–655.

12. http://www.crs.org/peacebuilding/index.cfm/&?utm_source=google-grant&utm_medium=cpc&utm_campaign=peacebuilding&gclid=CMbp5fLTjLECFdOa7QodBiCv_A, accessed July 9, 2012

PART III:

Limits, the Future, and Exercises

7

Limits of Collegial Ethics

However beautiful the strategy, you should occasionally look at the results. —Winston Churchill[1]

A collegial group is one in which the lines of communication are open, where help is offered, where individuals are appreciated, and where compassion and empathy are found. Also, it is a group in which individuals make an effort to practice and develop collegial skills. But it no doubt has occurred to you that collegiality is sometimes not as easy as it sounds. An obvious problem could be that someone spurns collegiality, or that collegial activity somehow creates a problem. There are other limitations to collegiality as well.

Unwilling and Unworthy Colleagues

Sometimes it just doesn't seem possible to support a colleague. It may be that something horrendous has been done, and there's no doubt that the colleague is responsible. This is usually an extreme case, and we let the courts or others deal with that problem. A resolution may require incarceration and a lengthy rehabilitation. In a sense, we can support such an individual, but it would be by pushing for and supporting a safe and effective rehabilitation. Fortunately, these situations are rare.

Sometimes we meet colleagues who simply aren't interested in being collegial. They may never tell you why, and they may not even know why. We can invite, but we can't force participation in the process of being collegial. But we can be model citizens of our community and that may attract people. People have different personalities and the outgoing and highly interactive are the ones we see and feel the most. There are also the introverts, those who do best when alone, and they may be collegial in their own way. Real collegiality has to accommodate everyone, but it may be expressed in different ways.

Do we support somebody who does not like or support us? Maybe they constantly belittle and undermine us, especially behind our back. It is generous to support others whether or not they like us. But there are limits; if others are destructive to us, it may be that giving support may give the wrong impression. We may lead them to believe that we support and accept their ideas and approach when we definitely do not. It could fuel their destructive tendencies. It is useful to explain to such a colleague where you stand on this, and give him or her another chance. But it is obviously not wise to support that which is destructive to us.

We may find colleagues who act in a way such that we don't feel comfortable giving blanket support to them. For example, we may find colleagues who use relationships to achieve their own personal gain and use collegiality to manipulate others. They cultivate liking and support in the hopes of getting something for themselves, such as free help or the opportunity to sell something. This is no interest in reciprocation; rather the goal is self-service without a thought of others or a pang of conscience. They may not see any problem with this behavior, which in the extreme is sociopathic. Sociopathic behavior is found at all levels of society. A reasonable approach is to try to enlighten these colleagues in the hope that with time they will be able to behave less selfishly. In the meantime, we need to be aware of and careful of these people. Perhaps their agenda can also be mutually positive for you and others, but clearly that cannot always be a given. No one likes to be used.

Protect Yourself

As noted in the previous paragraph, being supportive and fair can make you more vulnerable to the abuse of others. It seems worthwhile to amplify this a little. Sociopaths, for example, referred to in the previous paragraph, have no conscience and easily exploit others. A recent book by Martha Stout[2], a clinical psychologist, discusses at length what sociopaths are like and what we need to do about it. This is a significant problem, because according to this source, they are found in 4% of the population, or about one in twenty-five. It seems certain that all of us have at least met one or routinely interact with one.

Sociopaths are chillingly different from someone disposed to collegiality. They just aren't the same as the rest of us. They may do something that hurts somebody and they don't even notice, much less feel guilty. Their brain waves are different.[3] Some are financially successful, and some are not. Some are attractive, and some are not. But they are often charming and maybe seem like the nicest guy. The key weapon or tool that sociopaths use to survive and remain in our good graces is to elicit pity and empathy. So be aware that consistently irresponsible and apparently inadequate behavior, along with plays for our pity and sympathy, are warning signs that we may be dealing with sociopathic behavior. But worse, because collegiality fosters sympathy and forgiveness, we may be facilitating behavior that is destructive to us. We may be our own worst enemy. Some of the more collegial skills can make us vulnerable to being abused. Watch out for this!

How do we protect ourselves? Stout recommends staying away from people who repeatedly break our trust and the social contract. Three strikes and you are out. For our own sake, collegiality has to have its limits.

At some point we need to address bizarre behavior, which we sometimes see in our colleagues. Consider some unlikely event such as colleagues breaking into your home or office and going through your things, and maybe even planting fake evidence of wrongdoing, for whatever reasons. Suppose further that they lie to you when confronted and deny such activities. The exact event is not important here; one could imagine many kinds of bizarre occurrences and behaviors. But surely one would wonder about such colleagues. Do they have an appropriate sense of boundaries? Do they have a conscience? Is such risky behavior at all sensible? But the question is what should you do about these strange and unlikely behaviors of others? Should you be thinking about getting police or suggesting counseling? What would these colleagues with strange behavior have to do before you could write a letter of recommendation for them? If you are a superior or supervisor of the involved parties, how would you decide whether or not to intervene and what would you do?

Not All Colleagues Are Healthy and Able

Some colleagues are wounded and insecure and may need personal development and healing before they can be generous to others. Some individuals in our environment have underlying illnesses, either physical or emotional. Someone who is fighting cancer may not have the energy for new collegial relationships or commitments. Someone suffering from acute depression may not be very responsive to others until the depression is resolved. Someone who is a recovering alcoholic may not want to join you for lunch where alcohol is served—and the individual may not want to reveal that. Someone may not want to enter into a helping relationship if it conjures up memories of painful losses that the person is not ready to accept. There may be extenuating circumstances, and people are not always ready and able to get involved. So if someone avoids new collegial involvements, it may be a wise thing and not an irresponsible or inconsiderate response.

Collegiality vs. Appropriate Self-Interest

How do we meld collegiality with appropriate competitiveness, debate, and investigation of wrongdoing? In some cases helping others may need to be limited in some way. In many professions competitiveness is essential and is built into the structure of the job and career. We must act competitively in order to survive. Every salesman has the same right to try to sell his wares to a person or group as every other salesman. In the courtroom, the lawyer for the defense has to keep his client's best interest at heart and compete with the prosecutor. If we are investigating the wrongdoing of a colleague, we have to set aside collegiality and proceed in a mode where fact gathering and judgments are primary and essential. A general in the war is trained to respond to a military situation and has the welfare of his nation at heart. Accordingly, he must dictate strategy and tactics to subordinates even though they may be injured or possibly even lose their lives.

But, fortunately, what to do and the position to take, in at least some of these cases, are obvious. For instance, generals and prosecutors must do their jobs for the sake of the well-being of their communities, and we need to support them. But perhaps at least some collegiality can still be maintained in these situations in the sense that fairness must be maintained. For example, when investigating wrongdoing, you would not plant false evidence or leak damaging facts to the press. In the courtroom, while you must defend or prosecute the accused according to your role, it can be done fairly and according to the standards of the law and of your profession.

Consider the following complex but realistic situation. Suppose you are committed to going to a professional school and have made a great effort in that direction already. You have taken a lot of the required courses, and your advisors have said that if you continue to succeed, they will recommend you. Now further suppose that you are taking a course that is recognized as being essential to admission to the professional school and that getting an A usually guarantees a recommendation while a B puts you in a weaker position. Further suppose that the teacher of this course announces that only 40 percent of the class will get As or Bs and the rest will get Cs or worse. This teacher has had this policy for years in spite of some complaints. You are very aware that to get an A you will have to show your mastery of the subject, and getting an A is very important. So before the final exam, which counts for 60 percent of the grade, you work diligently on possible exam questions and you feel ready. You are an independent self-starter and have prepared well. Being a self-starter and preparing well are qualities that are highly prized by the professional schools that you are interested in. Now here comes a problem. Three classmates come to you and ask for help. They are not doing well in the course and have not prepared for the exam, and they want your help and direction. They ask you about likely exam questions and how to answer them. What are you justified in doing? Do you diligently help them and risk being less competitive for an A? Or do you make an excuse and send them away, maybe saying you haven't yet studied? Or do you offer some direction without giving over everything you know? You have been doing your job as a student and you deserve your fair grade. But, how much time should you give to others who have not yet done the work but want the fruits of your efforts? What do you think? You want to do something to help, but you also feel conflicted. Do you feel that you have to be fair and just to yourself first?

There are situations that are gray areas, and deciding how to be both collegial and appropriately self-interested may not be easy. Trying to have both could easily produce personal or societal conflict. But we can hope that, by being aware of both collegiality *and* of our own self interest, we will at least have an enlightened form of conflict—enlightened in the sense that we are aware of the competing interests and prepared to do or to change what we do as the situation develops. It's often the best we can do.

Are Right and Wrong Always Obvious?

Many want to say yes to this question. But it seems that there are situations where right and wrong are not always obvious. It may depend on where you stand in a given situation or on the outcome of decisions that are not always predictable. You could say that what provides the greatest benefit for the largest number is good. Or you could take a more personal view and say that everyone should use the golden rule, and what is kind to us personally is what is good.

What do we do when we are in doubt? There are no simple rules for this, and it will depend on the situation and the judgments made. Caution is clearly called for when the impact of our actions is uncertain. Mistakes will be made because human beings make mistakes, but we can hope that fewer mistakes will be made when we are aware of all of our options. If doing *no* harm is not possible, we should try at least try to *minimize* harm. Collegial ethics tends to place collegiality and support among the highest of our values. It also tends to place mercy least as high as punishment and to give colleagues the benefit of the doubt. This has been discussed in more detail in chapter 4.

Hierarchical Issues

Hierarchical issues are those that exist when elements in different levels of a hierarchy interact—for example, an employee and his boss or a citizen and his government. The authority of all levels of the hierarchy is not the same. Higher levels are sanctioned to do more, and they have more power and authority than lower levels. If you thought someone committed a horrendous crime and you personally punished him or her, then you could be a vigilante and lawbreaker and you would be punished. But if that person were tried and convicted, then a punishment by society would be warranted. If you took a job away from someone sitting at the next desk, it would be inappropriate, but if your employer laid off that person because of difficult economic times, then everyone would go along with it. Thus the acceptable standards and even the goals for different levels of a hierarchy can be different. This has been appreciated for many years. In the early 1930s, Reinhold Niebuhr, a Catholic theologian, said the same in his book *Moral Man and Immoral Society*.[4] He said that the morality of groups and individuals is different. The individual might respond to an appeal from reason and justice, but, in his view, groups usually defend their economic interests first.

This power disparity in hierarchies can be a complication for collegial ethics. If your co-worker is being laid off, even if apparently unjustly, it is difficult for you to do anything if it will threaten your own position in the organization. Perhaps the best you can do for that co-worker is listen, be compassionate, and provide some practical help. The latter could include helping with a new resume or getting a lead on a new position or a new direction, if these are not provided for. Seeing power and moral differences is easy in the cases described. But, what about situations that are more subtle? Will a poor person view a rich person as having more power and therefore not expect equality? Status differences, real or perceived, can affect our expectations and our actions with colleagues. Whatever the hierarchical differences might be, we still need to strive for collegiality in those situations.

Consider the case of a boss in a bind. Dr. Bind is in charge of a large department and is doing well. Unexpectedly, he has been told by his superior to "get rid of" a certain professional employee, Dr. X, who is viewed as threatening to the higher administration. But Dr. Bind knows that Dr. X hasn't committed any offense, certainly none that would warrant dismissal i. If anything, Dr. X appears threatening for reasons that have nothing to do with him personally. Dr. Bind feels a strong loyalty to his superior who recruited him, and Bind wants to keep him satisfied. He also worries that if he doesn't get rid of Dr. X, there may be subtle retaliations such as getting fewer resources and approvals from his boss, which would affect everyone. Nevertheless he and other staff members sense that this is not a simple, proper request but more of a political one.

What can Dr. Bind do? It seems that he could carry out his superior's wishes and force Dr. X out of his job. But he will have to live with having committed an action that is difficult to justify. Another risk is that he will be viewed, and appropriately so, as unfair and as an administrative puppet. This could have repercussions and affect his career. But most of all, Dr. Bind does not want to be unethical. But he also realizes that if he doesn't get rid of Dr. X, someone else might.

Assuming that those who have the greatest power and authority also have the greatest responsibility, Dr. Bind decides to work with his boss and try to show how dangerous the action could be. This is a good solution. He will examine the reasons behind the request, and then try to show that they are not worthy of that action. He can ask for the documentation of the failures of Dr. X. Any punishment given must match the transgression. If the failures don't justify the action, then he can try to explain that the request is not completely rational. He can point out how bad decisions made today can have ramifications for a long time to come.

Are We Equal Or Not?

Even the Declaration of Independence says we are equal, but how are we equal? In what ways? We clearly aren't equal in the way we perform, because, for example, the Olympics allow for only one gold medal. The others get lesser medals or none at all. Not everybody has the skill and experience to be the boss. So we are not equal in our ability to perform in certain arenas, and some do it better than others. But maybe the best way to view equality is that we are all *intrinsically* equal with the same very basic rights. At least acting that way helps guarantee opportunities and dignity for all.

Secrecy and Lying

In some cases, secrecy is part of a job. Working for the FBI or CIA comes to mind as an example of this, but there are many others. Information in personnel files, letters of recommendation and medical records are all confidential. Secrecy often exists for our own protection and is a fact of life. You may not be able to share problems or issues that arise when it is covered by a secrecy agreement. Hopefully, the requirement for secrecy provides a greater benefit than if the information was public. While secrecy and confidentiality must be respected, we can still respect collegiality.

Lying[5] can be a bad habit, simply a way to avoid an uncomfortable moment and embarrassment. In these cases, it cannot always be justified. But, lying can also be a way to minimize harm and protect someone. A doctor may tell a seriously suicidal patient that he might live years and that research is always finding new cures for his illness—when he knows from his experience that the patient likely has only a few months to live. You may say that you don't know where someone is to protect the person from harm. In extreme situations, you may lie to survive a serious threat. Lying may also be required to protect a necessary confidentiality. Lying seems to be a fact of life, perhaps more than it needs to be, but it nevertheless is. As you would expect, lying has been discussed over the centuries. The philosopher Immanuel Kant felt that no lie is permissible. But the Utilitarians, another group of philosophers, felt that lying was acceptable if it produced more good than harm.[6] Perhaps the outcome or impact of the lie will be the most important factor in judging it. Sifting truths from lies is part of judging the situation, as described in chapter 4.

When is a lie *not* justified? Some examples of lies that are *not* acceptable are those that cause destructive results that could have been avoided, lying under oath, lying to avoid responsibility for an action, or lying simply because you felt like it. It seems best to avoid a lie unless you can't for some reason. Note that collegial discussions can be had without going into all confidential details (for example, the case in chapter 5 where a senior person talks with younger colleagues at a coffee shop but doesn't ask for all the details or names). Lying to colleagues is not a good idea unless it is mutually understood that some information is being withheld or faked to facilitate a conversation. Keep a log of how often and under what circumstances you lie. Will you be surprised at the results?

Access To Training In Collegial Ethics Could Be A Problem

Many people likely have not been fully exposed to collegial ethics. Fortunately, in this day and age, we can obtain encyclopedic knowledge simply by having Internet access. It seems that all that is needed is real interest and some time for collegial ethics. Collecting cases and finding discussion and role-playing groups may be somewhat more difficult. Mentoring as described in a former chapter is essential. Introducing young colleagues to collegial ethics will be important to give the culture of collegial ethics a long life and continued growth.

The Bottom Line

The goal of collegial ethics is to support our colleagues in various ways, to advise, and to show compassion. However, there are limits to this. Some colleagues are unwilling or unworthy, and not all of them are physically or emotionally able. Sometimes being collegial conflicts with our own self-interest; we have to decide the best course of action. Hierarchical problems, secrecy, lying, and the complexity of right vs. wrong can be difficult issues. Learning collegiality is easier if quality mentoring is available.

Notes for Chapter 7

1. Winston Churchill. From http://en.thinkexist.com/quotes/like/genius_has_limitations-stupidity_is/185796/4.html, accessed July 23, 2012.

2. M. Stout. *The Sociopath Next Door* (New York: Three Rivers Press, 2005).

3. J. Intrator et al., "A Brain Imaging (SPECT) Study of Semantic and Affective processing in Psychopaths," *Biol Psychiat* 42 (1997): 96-103.

4. R. Niebuhr, *Moral Man and Immoral Society* (Louisville: Westminster John Knox Press, 1932).

5. S. Bok, *Lying: Moral Choice in Public and Private Life*, 2nd Ed. (New York, Vintage Books, 1999).

6. Summarized from http://www.scu.edu/ethics/publications/iie/v6n4/lying.html, accessed August 16, 2012

8

Synthesis and Exercises

The future depends on what you do today.
—Mahatma Gandhi[1]

Collegial ethics proposes that we support our colleagues (again, some prefer the word "co-workers") and be fair to them whenever we can, exhibiting compassion and empathy and developing the skills to do so. Collegial ethics is needed because we interact with colleagues all the time yet get little or no training or guidance in how best to handle these interactions. Practicing collegial ethics will improve all of our lives in many ways.

List Of Collegial Principles

- When interacting with colleagues, be uplifting, supportive, compassionate, and helpful whenever you can. Devote some time to the interaction, listen attentively, and reflect before responding. As these skills spread, our world will become a better one.
- Devote some *time* to learning the skills associated with collegial ethics. These skills include practicing an effective and fair style of language, using the golden rule and doing least

harm, learning to handle conflict, and mentoring others. A reasonable learning approach is to study the principles of collegial ethics, to discuss cases and relevant principles in groups, to practice the skills required, and to discuss again the outcome of your actions.

- Be aware that our tendencies and automatic responses to colleagues and situations are part of human nature, but they are not always rational and useful to us. There are many questionable ways that we use to convince ourselves to do nothing and avoid helping. Studying and being aware of these tendencies and responses is a first step in freeing ourselves from them and developing new options for ourselves.
- We can learn new skills.[2] We *can change*.
- Develop judgment and courage. Sometimes supporting others and helping is very easy, but at other times it is more questionable. We have to make our decisions based on careful judgment and evaluation. We may need courage to act. We can have the best judgment, the right experience, and excellent interpersonal skills, but unless we act, all of that is wasted. Courage seems critical and needs to be developed.
- Utilize language that shows fairness and does no (intended) harm. Learn how to use the language style that resolves issues most effectively, communicates your needs very clearly, anticipates the needs of others, and avoids moral judgments, comparisons, and righteousness.
- Giving credit to others is a highly nourishing and supportive act. It is one of the best ways of being collegial.
- In conflicts, which are often normal and necessary, be aware of your habits and options, look for mutual needs, and search for the win-win solution.
- Being collegial can make you vulnerable to those who might take advantage of you (for example, sociopaths). Preserve

and protect yourself. Someone who repeatedly misuses your kindnesses might best be avoided.
- Learn and practice enough that you can be an effective mentor to others. Mentoring is a gift to both the mentor and the mentee.

Questions For Discussion

The answers to the following twelve questions are useful for summarizing the contents of this book.

1. Describe a collegial community. How do people interact? How can competition and debate exist in such a community?
2. Think of a situation or situations in your life where collegial interactions have been a problem. What exactly is the root of the problem? How can you address it?
3. Sometimes we *like* colleagues and sometimes we don't. In what kinds of relationships is liking important? In collegial relationships, what is more important, liking a colleague or behaving appropriately according to the goals of your group?
4. Human nature is an important topic for collegial ethics. Many times we react automatically to situations, and these automatic reactions have likely benefited us in many instances, particularly in ancestral times. But they are not always advantageous when dealing with colleagues. Discuss some studies that reveal aspects of human behavior that can affect interactions with others. Do we sometimes act automatically or intuitively and then afterwards righteously justify the actions with moral judgments?
5. When confronted with a collegial opportunity, how do you decide or judge how you should deal with it? What are the factors in deciding how active you should be? What is forecasting?
6. Courage is often the forgotten factor in using our knowledge and skills. Without courage, our judgment, knowledge, experience, and skills can be wasted. How can we *develop*

greater courage? Please spend time on this one because it seems very important.
7. Sometimes hierarchies complicate collegiality. For example, sometimes there are issues between a subordinate and a superior. What are the limitations in these situations? What are reasonable expectations of both sides? Are there limitations on obedience to authority?
8. Make a list of collegial skills that focus on language, the platinum rule, and doing least harm. Include detraction, which is the needless revealing of embarrassing past events of others. Discuss an example of how each could be used. Practice language styles that are supportive and avoid judgments, righteousness, comparisons, and denials of responsibility.
9. In nonviolent communication (NVC), there is a focus on listening, discovering feelings and needs, and making appropriate requests. How would you help and direct a colleague who is very angry—almost helplessly angry—at another colleague?
10. In conflict resolution (CR), arriving at a win-win solution is critical. What does that mean? Is conflict normal, natural, neutral, and necessary, and what does that imply? What are the various styles for dealing with conflict? Describe helpful styles of communication.
11. Collegiality has its limits, inherent or imposed. Discuss them. Some aspects of a situation are not under your control, but some require you to decide what is in your best interest.
12. Can you think of other topics that are important for collegial ethics that are not discussed in this book? Which ones are important in *your* life?

Language Styles

It is possible to develop a language style that is supportive and generous at best and benign at worst. Some cases in the previous chapters illustrate this language style.

The cafeteria talk in chapter 5 describes how two different discussions of the same topic can sound and how a listener might be influenced by each one. Avoiding premature judgments and avoiding being righteous make for a better environment. The case in chapter 1 describing an erroneous charge of fabricating data is an example of keeping your head when you talk. Be careful to distinguish what you see from what you think it means. Please reread these cases and the related discussion.

In this exercise recall a recent conversation in which an individual was trashed, perhaps demonized? Can you replay that conversation using a more generous and supportive attitude toward the person, and language that is more benign? What are the reasons for being judgmental and righteous? What are the reasons to be supportive and kind?

Listening For Feelings and Needs and Making Requests

Sometimes when we have exchanges with colleagues (coworkers) that are emotional, we're more interested in having the last word or the cleverest word, rather than solving the problem. This may not help and in fact may make things worse. The material in the first part of chapter 6 focuses on this. One effective approach to solving problems is to use an approach that focuses on the feelings and needs of the involved parties. The case of stealing ideas is summarized here.

Supposing a colleague, Ray, is fuming with anger. He says, "Fred over there really upsets me. He seems to be running to the boss with my ideas all the time. I've been giving him dirty looks, and I swear at him when I pass his desk, but he just hasn't gotten the idea. He continues to go to the boss with my ideas and makes it look like they are his."

You might say to him, "Ray, have you told him directly what your feelings and needs are?" Ray could be coached so that his responses, needs, and feelings are clear to him, and you could also encourage him to state clearly what he wants from Fred.

You could suggest that he have a discussion with Fred in which Ray might say, "Fred, I've been upset. I feel like you go to the boss with my ideas, which makes me feel that you have no respect for me as a colleague. I'm just like everyone else and I need to have my contributions recognized. Maybe because of your enthusiasm for this work, you aren't aware of what you are doing to me. I was hoping that you would not do this anymore, or at least give me the opportunity to talk to the boss about my own ideas. At the very least I feel you should give me the credit I need when you talk to him." No matter what the response of the colleague might be, it is clear that this kind of expression is much more informative. It states what's happening, describes his feelings, presents his needs, and makes a specific request (the four components). It employs the word "I" which shows responsibility for his feelings. Of course, all of this should be said in a very sincere way. Saying these things by yelling or belittling your colleague in front of others can only make the situation worse. The colleague might come back and say that he was sorry, or he may have information that shows you are not entirely correct. If both colleagues communicate using the four components of NVC, they are more likely to reach a mutual understanding.

Practice using the four components in emotionally charged situations.

Which of the following statements conveys precise information and makes a precise rather than vague request which is a collegial skill?

1. I'd like you to come home by 7:00 p.m. at the latest and help me put the children to bed.
2. Can't you get home earlier?
3. I need your draft of the report by noon this Friday because my deadline is 5:00 p.m, and I need several hours to complete my part and make sure we agree.
4. Get it to me as soon as you can.

5. I'm upset about what you said an hour ago because it made me look lazy and not caring. I had a good reason for being late with the material, and you should have asked me about it before denigrating me to everyone in the office.
6. Damn you. Don't talk about me like that ever again.
7. I know you don't like me, but we don't always like everyone we work with. We both work here and have the same goals, so let's focus on that. Please leave personal issues out of the process because they just create problems and disrupt productivity.
8. I know you don't like me, and I really don't care for you. Maybe you should leave. Everyone here likes me, not you.

The odd-numbered statements are more precise, informative, collegial and less likely to cause interpersonal problems. If the reply you get is also precise and informative, you are likely to have a productive conversation.

Win-Win

Another important approach in addressing conflicts is to find the win-win solution. Conflict cannot be avoided in life, and if we get used to that idea, we won't be so aversive to conflict. A good way to be less afraid of conflict is to prepare for it and to consider it a challenge. Again, we go back to discovering everyone's wants and needs, particularly the latter, and trying to find a solution that allows everyone to get something: a win-win solution.

Chapter 6 describes the five very different response styles to conflict. They include competing, accommodating, avoiding, collaborating, and compromising. List some conflicts that have troubled you, and next to each one, list your style of response. Consider the style called avoiding. Have you avoided dealing with your conflicts? If the avoidance is not founded on fear and aversion of conflict, this could be reasonable if the problem is minor or if the solution is too costly to be implemented. Do you insist that it has to be done your way? Perhaps you are correct and you have the expertise to feel comfortable with this response. But maybe it is not getting you anywhere and maybe you can benefit from a change in response style. Are you willing to compromise, which usually means that all sides give up something? Are you willing to collaborate and search sincerely for a solution? Think of new or different approaches to the conflicts. Spend some time with this because it can create new, interesting, and rewarding ideas.

Courage

In chapter 4 it says that we can have wide-ranging experiences, sound judgment, and great moral foundation, but unless we know how *to act* on an issue, *all that is wasted*. Sometimes it is clear that we should act but we don't, and chapters 2 and 3 cover some of the reasons why we might not. This is where the very important ingredient of *courage* comes into play. It is often the critical and missing factor in many ethical situations and one of the most important skills in collegiality. How do we develop it?

Developing courage starts in small ways. Stand up to a bullying colleague. Express your concern when someone is demonized. Try to stop a destructive occurrence by acting. Focus on the good outcome of your actions instead of the negative ones. Read about courageous people and their acts. Build up a personal culture of courage. Write down situations in which you felt like you weren't courageous enough. Make a list of comments or actions that you could have used that were courageous. This is important: in detail, list the good that would have resulted from your courage. Search out people who are interested in courage, and support each other. Can you think of other ways to develop courage? Spend some time on this critical issue.

Cases and Questions

A Distressed Colleague

A colleague in your group has recently lost his wife and child in an automobile accident. Needless to say, he is severely depressed and barely functional, even months after the event. Your group has been working on an important project for your company, and the project has a hard deadline. Your distressed colleague really can't contribute, and this puts stress on everyone else in the group. Your boss is beside herself and needs additional manpower to help. She comes to you and asks what you think should be done. What are the topics you need to address in this conversation? Is it medical care needed for your colleague? Is it a recitation of his excellent past performance? Is it a search for a way to get temporary help to get the job done without discarding the colleague? Should he be let go? Do you get a medical opinion about his prognosis? Or maybe you need to address many of these? Are some people making an attribution error and thinking that they would do much better than the widower?

Human tendencies that won't be helpful in the situation are to avoid the distressed person, to assume that others will help him and that you aren't needed, or to blame the person for continuing to be in mourning when he should have "snapped out of it" weeks ago.

Boss Who Verbally Trashes His Employees

There are many wonderful bosses in the world, and they are appreciated. Sometimes it not easy being the boss, and they need support. But we've all seen the boss who verbally belittles and demeans employees, usually behind their back. Consider the following scenario.

Mark is an employee who has had some bad luck in his job. Things haven't gone well for him since he started, but he is making a solid effort to get things going well and to do well. Just about all his colleagues feel that the failures were not his fault, and they give him the needed collegial support.

But his boss, who has been successful in his job, makes verbal cracks about Mark that belittle him to his senior staff. He repeats things Mark says in a mocking way while laughing. "I'm going to make it work" he repeats in a sing-song manner with a mocking tone while shaking his head. He laughs about things Mark says even thought they aren't really funny. Moreover he shuns Mark as though he was useless and shows little respect for him. People are becoming aware that he does it to other subordinates as well.

Why does the boss do this? Is it a bad habit? Is it a way to avoid giving Mark some extra help so he can do better? Is it his way of "lightening up" in the face of problems? Does he genuinely despise underlings who appear weak? Does he have some of the traits of a bully?

What should his senior staff do in response to these actions? What are the strategies they can use to get him to change his behavior? Mark finds out about it. What strategies can Mark use to be treated better and to get the respect that employees who are in difficult situations deserve? Maybe showing the boss how his actions hurt himself and the organization would be a place to start.

A Mistaken Accusation

Dr. V is a researcher interested in how medicines such as antidepressants and addictive drugs affect the brain. This is a critical problem involving a large amount of resources. He recently did something very useful: he developed a procedure that showed where these drugs acted in the brain. He combined existing experimental procedures into a newer one that avoided the pitfalls of the existing ones. It was a significant advance, one that allowed many new studies of the brain and its response to medications. A colleague of Dr. V, Dr. C, knew about the work and had previously worked with Dr. V. Accordingly, as a courtesy, Dr. V sent a copy of the procedure to Dr. C well before it was published and available to everyone.

But Dr. C, for whatever reason, attacked the paper, saying that not all of the proper citations were included. Because of this, Dr. V was added to a list of people to be sanctioned or investigated. This action caused much trouble for Dr. V and great emotional distress, especially because the citations were in fact included in the paper but apparently had been missed by Dr. C.

When Dr. C discovers her mistake, what are her ethical obligations to Dr. V and everyone else? Should she take advantage of Dr. V's vulnerable position and publish her own work on the topic? Should she concoct lies that support her error? Or should she assist Dr. V in his distress? She may say that some of this is Dr. V own fault; but, even if partly true, what are her ethical obligations and responsibilities regarding her error?

The Whistle-blower

Dr. Jean White is a senior faculty member who has been very successful. She has built an effective program that brings in many millions of federal dollars per year. Everything is going very well until she discovers that one of her subordinates has been embezzling funds from the program. The dollar amount is not trivial, and Dr. White becomes very worried about what to do. She considers doing nothing and working it out within her group, but then she worries that she may be guilty of a cover-up or of breaking some other federal rule. Because the money stolen is from a federal grant, she is concerned about penalties at the federal level, and she wants to do the right thing.

She decides that the only way to keep her and her program out of jeopardy and to keep everything moving forward is to report the crime to her superiors and to the federal unit providing the funds. She does so, and a very thorough investigation follows (even Dr. White is investigated) and Dr. White is vindicated. The embezzler is sent to prison, but, unfortunately, the university is embarrassed and has to repay some funds. The entire process takes some years to complete.

During the investigation and afterward, Dr. White was shunned by long-time friends and associates and was gossiped about relentlessly. She lost control of the program that she so successfully developed and led, was moved to a less prestigious position, and was pressured to take early retirement. Some of her friends even condemned her actions. All of this happened because, through no fault of her own, someone embezzled funds and she blew the whistle and tried to keep her reputation and program intact.

Unfortunately, this kind of treatment of whistle-blowers is not uncommon and is a significant problem. How can collegial ethics improve the lot of whistle-blowers? Would the university be justified in telling everyone to avoid Dr. White until the situation is resolved? Avoidance of people in difficult positions is very common. What could be the reason? In order to overcome this tendency, what would you do or what skills would you practice? Also, discuss how the following topics might apply here: attribution errors, self-righteousness, and moralistic judgments.

Director Rook and Mr. Nubie

A new senior employee, Mr. Nubie, arrives on-site. He has had some professional problems with his colleagues in the past, and some of those who attacked Mr. Nubie got in trouble. He is hoping to put those problems and relationships behind him in his new job. He is enthusiastic and plans to be successful.

About the same time, a new director, Mr. Rook, is appointed, and one of Mr. Nubie's previous enemies, someone who was previously dismissed for an inappropriate attack, calls the director and tells the director about his problems with Mr. Nubie. It turns out that he leaves out significant details, which the director doesn't realize. Perhaps the director knows and likes the caller and sides

Synthesis and exercises **141**

with him. In any case, he decides that Mr. Nubie has to go. What should the director do next?

Here are some options:

1. The director tells others around the site that he thinks Mr. Nubie should leave, hoping Nubie will hear that and leave on his own accord. But Nubie hears the rumors about the Director's unhappiness and confronts him about the rumors. Unfortunately, the director denies them and then sometimes laughs at Nubie behind his back.
2. The director tries to involve others and asks them to get Mr. Nubie to leave any way that they can.
3. The director speaks to Mr. Nubie privately, explains the situation and his feelings, and tells him that he wants him to leave. He is willing to listen to Mr. Nubie, but his mind may be made up. Even though the director feels the situation is difficult, he gives Mr. Nubie the dignity he deserves and the opportunity to explain his side of the story.
4. Obviously, option 3, or a similar version, is the only reasonable possibility. The others are somewhat immature, disrespectful, and deny Mr. Nubie an opportunity to reply and rebut the charges.
5. Discuss how the following factors could be involved in this case: disliking vs. liking, demonization, detraction, hierarchies, courage, the platinum rule, righteous judgments, and avoiding conflict.

Employee vs. Boss Conflict

A company has an employee who has been involved in a problem that was not very attractive for the company and left it in a very nonflattering light. One of the company's products was thought to be defective, and while the company felt it was not a big problem, a significant recall resulted that the company considered controversial. The employee was one who pushed for the recall before the leadership was ready for it, and he or she is now considered disloyal and having questionable judgment.

Some of the leadership of the company feels incensed by the mere presence of the employee and feels that he or she and reminds them about the controversy, and wishes that he or she would move on to another job. Other company leaders do not quite see this point of view, feeling that the employee was loyal in his or her own way and fought for what he or she thought was best for the company. The employee has been working in good faith and feels invested in the company, and also feels that moving on would result in professional and personal losses as well as a stigma of failure that is not deserved. The company has not offered any kind of compensation to the employee to make up for the losses he or she would endure.

The president of the company, who has grown to dislike the employee, never misses an opportunity to demean the employee. He calls the employee "our traitor" or "our troublemaker" to his staff. When the staff doesn't support his comment or doesn't respond positively to it, he pushes for agreement. He might say, "Oh, come on, you know how much trouble he caused us," and he does this in an expectant way, waiting for the others to agree. He pushes the issue until he gets some form of agreement. He is nearly belligerent about it, but he is the president and few argue with him. He doesn't seriously consider a separation package because he says he can't afford it, and that the company would be hurt by one. But members of his staff disagree in private and say that some kind of package should be given and could be afforded. But nothing has been done and the president continues to consider the employee as a problem to be gotten rid of. He praises the members of his staff who make disparaging comments about him and he seems to derive energy and justification from these negative comments. Whenever the employee does something that many others might do, he is singled out for criticism by the president and by those wanting to please the president.

Let us examine this situation from several points of view. Rereading chapters 2 to 5 would be helpful for identifying human tendencies present in all of us that we need to be aware of.

First, the president is fixed in his view, hasn't softened, and insists that his staff forms the same opinions about the employee. One possibility is that he really believes that the recalled product was fine but that the company was pushed into the recall by people like the employee. Maybe he believes that those against the product didn't have the credentials to judge it. Further, he is insisting on loyalty from his staff and defines that as agreeing with him. What can we say about his motives and position? Well it seems that he is armoring himself against the idea that there was a problem with the product. He wants to blame others for the recall. Is he having a problem with being open minded? Does his insisting on loyalty have any problems? Could a personal dislike of the employee be a factor here, and is that appropriate? Is he demonizing the employee? Is he aware of his power of authority and how many obey authority no matter what? Is he practicing the golden rule, and is he showing belief in the idea of "first do no harm?" If he would listen to you, what would you say to the president of the company?

Second, the president's staff is under pressure here, although there are some who also agree with the president about the employee and always have. Are they aware of how authority can elicit obedience (Milgram's experiments) even when someone may be unnecessarily hurt? Are they experiencing a subconscious pressure to agree with the boss because they want to be part of the community of the company? Are they afraid of losing at least the favor of the president and perhaps their job? How could those staff members who disagree with the president's behavior help the president? Could they ask him to consider the long term consequences of his views and actions on morale or future issues? They might point out that the president needs to be careful because unfair behavior on his part might be remembered into the future. Also, his behavior may be calling attention to the situation.

The third point of view is the employee's. Should the employee tolerate this situation? Should he get what he can and leave? What if no other company will want him because of the "disloyal" label pinned on him by the president? What if he refuses to accept unfair treatment and insists on staying and working through the problem. If the president would listen to him, what should he say using a statement that includes feelings, needs and makes appropriate requests as described in NVC? What could the president say back to the employee using the same framework?

Is the last point of view the best one and what should happen? Well, this is difficult to say because there are so many variables. Overall, this does seem to be a problem that involves a hierarchy where there is an imbalance of power, which is not uncommon. What can both sides do to insure that they are behaving fairly with the other?

It Was My Fault

Suppose you injure someone, perhaps by making an erroneous decision about them. It could be that it caused the loss of a job, or serious damage to their reputation and income. Furthermore, the injured person is livid over his or her loss. This is a situation where it is tempting to run away and ignore the error you made. Maybe you can blame the victim to somehow justify your mistake and ignore your responsibility. Emotions aside, the collegial requirement (and general ethical requirement) is to make amends for your error as best you can. Hopefully the damage was not irreversible, but it could be. The reparation required has to match the damage done by you. What exactly could you do? The damage and restitution case in chapter 3 is an example of this problem.

There might be many good ways to deal with this. Maybe you should begin by explaining what happened and why the error occurred.

Was there a misunderstanding? Were you overcome with emotion and anger but now realize that that was inappropriate? Maybe you just weren't thinking. Maybe it wasn't totally your fault and some of the damage was due to an accident or unfortunate co-occurrence. Whatever you do, making amends for your part seems required. Can you fix it, or do you have to find another way to repay the error? Do you need to consult with a professional to feel OK about it?

Injuring someone can create many problems for you. You may feel guilty, lose confidence, and want to get away from the situation. A doctor who seriously injures a patient comes to mind. Unless dealt with in some way, it could have a negative impact on the doctor, his or her entire staff, and their future. Sometimes these are very difficult and troubling situations. Can you think of some general rules on how to deal with your injuries to others? Has there been a time when you were injured and it was appropriately dealt with. Or perhaps not?

Facing A Transition

You are part of a men's or women's group that meets regularly with the goal of maintaining relationships, supporting each other, and having fun. Some of the members are getting quite old, and one or two of them, not the oldest ones, are getting somewhat senile. They tend to ramble when they speak, and they sometimes ask others to repeat themselves a lot. But they clearly are not harmful, and they generally hold up their part in the group. What should your attitude toward them be?

Try to get them to leave the group before they become really infirm and a bigger problem. Maybe this could start by taking their email addresses off the contact list from time to time.

Ignore and belittle them at the group meeting, or maybe behind their backs so they aren't offended. This makes it easier to bear them.

Include and support them as regular members as best you can, and stay in touch with their friends and family so that consensus decisions could be made about their activities and living arrangements.

Number three is the best answer. Promoting human respect and dignity is the collegial path to take. It has been said that the way you treat the aging, is setting the model for how you will be treated as you age.

Do We Reveal The Past?

Suppose you discover some upsetting things about a colleague's past. Maybe the person committed a crime, or did something that led to a firing, or a demotion. Whatever it was, it was somehow dishonorable. What should you do? Do you have an obligation to make it known in the present? After all, it is the truth. Do you feel that the colleague is "hiding something and shouldn't get away with it?" Do you feel that if you ignore it, then you have to justify ignoring it? How do you approach this situation? Do you think about detraction (Chapter five)? While there may be many ways to approach this as a good colleague, maybe the following considerations suggest a reasonable path.

One consideration is whether or not the past event is having an effect in the present. Is the effect good or bad? If it is bad, will making the past known improve the present situation? Or will it make it worse?

Another issue is whether or not the colleague has made an effort to satisfy any ethical debt he/she may have incurred in the past. If damage was done to someone, have they been compensated in some manner by the colleague? If direct reimbursement wasn't possible, was there another approach, maybe giving to a charity, or performing community service, or maybe just regrets and new resolutions?

Has the colleague been on a good and honorable path ever since? Does she/he make an honest effort to be a good employee and a decent coworker? If you have questions, are you able to discuss them with the colleague privately? Maybe he/she has done the honorable thing after the transgression and has no debt.

Considering these issues will help you make up your mind. Collegial ethics generally proposes that past events in a person's life are not automatically relevant in the present. In fact, making known negative events from the past without good reason makes you a detractor, an injurer of someone's value, reputation and future. A detractor can rob all of us of the benefit and good deeds that the colleague may provide in the present and future. Also, who are we to judge? The saying of "judge not lest ye be judged" comes to mind.

Is the person "hiding" something? Well, maybe yes, and there is nothing wrong with it. There is nothing wrong with putting the past behind you and trying to be a model colleague today and tomorrow. In fact it is the collegial thing to do.

On some rare occasions, you may discover that a colleague has a continuing pattern of inappropriate behavior that damages others, from the past to the present. In that case, a different approach may be needed.

A Closing Word

This book, previous articles, and a website (collegialethics.com) strive to introduce collegial ethics, to examine the factors that underlie and affect this approach, and to outline a path for its implementation and practice. It will produce a better world for us. As noted below, collegiality is already around us, sometimes in bits and pieces and sometimes by another name. We need to harness and amplify that. There are also other likely and useful approaches and tools that are not described here, in addition to many illuminating cases that would be helpful to colleagues. This author would like to hear about those, or any other suggestions the reader may have.

Unexpectedly, a recent handout at a church service described the heart of collegial ethics.[3] The handout intended to summarize the church's view of healthy relationships.

"We will be mindful of how we communicate with others by:

Listening actively and seeking to understand; using 'I' statements when expressing our own views; being respectful and kind in our words, tone, and *body language; using e-mail and other forms of electronic communication with special care.*

We will seek peaceful and constructive resolutions to conflicts by: communicating directly with the person or group involved, instead of gossiping or speaking negatively about others in the wider community; assuming good intentions; checking the accuracy of our perceptions and assumptions; forgiving when people make mistakes; apologizing when warranted and seeking to make amends; calling on community* resources when help is needed."

Take a little time for collegiality, take it seriously, and take on the challenge of mastering helpful behaviors.

Notes for Chapter 8

1. Mahatma Gandhi, from http://www.goodreads.com/quotes/tag/future, accessed July 18, 2012

2. Nørgaard B, Ammentorp J, Kofoed PE, Kyvik KO: Training improves inter-collegial communication. *Clin Teach*; 9(3) (2012): 173-7

3. This is from the UUCA church service in Atlanta, GA, held on Sunday, September 9, 2012. * indicates a word change (from "congregation" to "community"). The original can be viewed at http://uuca.org/wp-content/uploads/2008/10/congregational_minutes_20080518.pdf, accessed on September 10, 2012. Permission to reproduce the text from this handout has been given by Rev Anthony David.

Supplemental Reading.

www.collegialethics.com

Alford, F. C. *Whistleblowers: Broken Lives and Organizational Power.* (Ithaca: Cornell University Press, 2001).

Arbinger Institute, *The Anatomy of Peace: Resolving the Heart of Conflict* (San Francisco: Berrett-Keohler, 2006).

Carlsmith, J. M. and L. Festinger. "Cognitive Consequences of Forced Compliance," *Journal of Abnormal and Social Psychology* 58 (1959): 203–210.

De Waal, F. *"The Bonobo and the Atheist: In Search of Humanism Among the Primates."* (New York, NY: W. W. Norton and Co Inc, 2013).

Gilbert, P. "The Evolved Basis and Adaptive Functions of Cognitive Distortions," *British Journal of Medical Psychology* 71 (1998): 447–463.

Gillespie, B. B. "No Jerks: Some Firms Argue That Collegiality Pays Off," *ABA Journal*, (March 1 issue), accessed on March 22, 2012, http://www.abajournal.com/magazine/article/no_jerks_some_firms_argue_that_collegiality_pays

Grant, Adam. *"Give and Take: A revolutionary Approach to Success."* (New York, NY: Penguin Group, 2013).

H.H. Dalai Lama (Author), Alexander Norman (Contributor). *Beyond Religion: Ethics for a Whole World* (NY, NY, Houghton Mifflin Harcourt Pub Co., 2011).

Haidt, Jonathan. *The Happiness Hypothesis: Finding Modern Truth in Ancient Wisdom.* (New York, NY. Basic Books, 2006).

Haidt, Jonathan. *The Righteous Mind: Why Good People Are Divided by Politics and Religion.* (New York, NY. Vintage Books, 2012)

Jagatic, K. and L. Keashly. "By Any Other Name: American Perspectives on Workplace Bullying," *Workplace Emotional Abuse Bullying and Emotional Abuse in the Workplace: International Perspectives in Research and Practice.* (London: Taylor Francis, 2003): 31–61.

Joy, Amy Block, *Whistleblower.* (Bay Tree Publishing: www.baytreepublish.com, 2010)

Keashly, L. and J. H. Neuman. "Reducing Aggression and Bullying: An Intervention Project in the US Department of Veterans Affairs," *Workplace Bullying: International Perspectives on Moving from Research to Practice.* Symposium conducted at the meeting of the Academy of Management, Honolulu, HI, August 2005.

Kurzban, R. and M. R. Leary. "Evolutionary Origins of Stigmatization: The Function of Social Exclusion," *Psychological Bulletin* 127 (2001): 187–208

Lachman, V.D. "Moral Courage: A Virtue in Need of Development?" *MedSurg Nursing Journal* 16(2) (2007): 131–133.

L. Leu, *Nonviolent Communication Companion Workbook* (Encinitas CA: Puddledancer Press, 2003).

C. W. Moore, *The Mediation Process: Practical Strategies for Resolving Conflict* (San Francisco: Jossey-Bass, 2006).

Nørgaard B, Ammentorp J, Kofoed PE, Kyvik KO: Training improves inter-collegial communication. *Clin Teach*; 9(3) (2012): 173-7

M. B. Rosenberg, *Nonviolent Communication: A Language of Life* (Encinitas CA: Puddledancer Press, 2003).

Silverman, F. H. *Collegiality and Service for Tenure and Beyond.* (Westport: Praeger Publishers, 2004.)

T. D. Wilson, *Redirect* (New York, NY: Little Brown and Company, 2011).

Index

apologies, 47, 86

attribution errors, 41

blacklisting, 13

bosses and Hierarchies, 67, 75, 79, 91, 99, 123-5, 131, 137, 141-2

bullying, 12, 45-7

bystander effect, 43-4

cases
    bad genes? 90-1
    blacklisting, 11
    boss in a bind, 124-5
    cafeteria trash talk, 74-5
    condolences, mentoring and do no harm, 5
    damage to others and restitution, 144-5
    dating boyfriend and disruption of office, 18-9
    distressed colleague, 137
    disrespectful email, 85
    employee vs. boss conflict, 141-2
    erroneous accusation of misconduct, 9, 11
    Genovese story, 43-4

Good Samaritan, 42
I can't stand that coworker, 23-5
kiss up to the boss, 99
making up data — really or not? 9, 88
mistaken accusation, 138
needy colleagues: me or them? 131-2
never-on-time colleague, 88-9
she's from a bad family, 90
stealing ideas, 97-8
trash talking boss, 137
trophy hire in question, 79-81, 140-1
to report or not to report, 83-5
the arguing couple, 108
whistleblower, 139

change behavior, 47-50, 130

collegial ethics
    costs, 6
    Defined, 3
    Implementing, 59-111
    Principles, 3, 129
    Skills, 71-111
    Usefulness, 4-13

compassion, 4, 18, 21, 32, 47, 60, 77, 81, 95, 104, 117, 129

competition, 8, 13, 75, 131

communication, 11, 73-5, 95-102, 108, 132-3, 137

conflict resolution, 92-100

courage, 5, 11, 29, 34, 64, 68, 76, 81-6, 129, 136-7

credit, giving, 86-7

Index

cultural factors, 44

Dale Carnegie, 65

damage to others, 47, 76, 81, 144

demonizing others, 11, 46, 76, 136

detraction, 81, 146-7

disliking vs. liking, 23-5, 47, 90

empathy, 4, 44, 47, 62, 77-8, 81, 95, 101, 107, 117, 129

ethical debt, 46-7, 62, 144-6

evolution - Influence on our actions, 29-33, 50

excessive fairness, 22

fairness, xiv, 3-5, 67, 91, 121-2

fear - paralyzing, 25

forgiveness, xv,

genes and heredity and behavior, 89-91

giving credit, 86-7

golden rule, 78

Good Samaritan study, 42

harm- do no or minimal harm, 45-6, 79-81, 123

hierarchies and bosses, see bosses

impact, 19-20, 33, 60, 73, 75, 83, 100

judgment, 5, 60-3, 123 129, 136

judgmental – see righteous and judgmental

language - destructive vs. supportive, 42, 72-6, 81, 95-110, 132

liking vs. disliking, 23-5, 47, 90

listening, 50, 60, 67, 77, 96, 101, 106, 129

lying, 126

mentoring, 19, 72, 87-91, 97, 111, 127, 129

nonviolent communication, 86-92

platinum rule, 78, 131

requests - Making, 96-8, 101, 107, 132-4

responsibility, 12, 44, 99-101, 144-5

responses
    automatic vs. thoughtful, 30-2
    rational or not, 38-9

restitution, 46-7, 144-5

reveal the past? 81, 146-7

Right vs. wrong, 123

righteous and judgmental, 21, 41, 66, 81, 132

saying it enhances belief, 42

secrecy, 126-7

self interest, 8-9, 121-3

sociopathic colleagues, 119

support, 3-5, 117-122,

time – to develop skills, 19, 38-9, 62, 74, 82, 103, 129

tolerance, 66-67

training in collegial ethics, 10, 36-7, 47-50, 71-2, 127

whistleblowing, 10-13, 139

win-win, 135